DR. FRANK FIELD'S GET OUT ALIVE

DR. FRANK FIELD'S
GET OUT
ALIVE

SAVE YOUR FAMILY'S LIFE
WITH FIRE SURVIVAL TECHNIQUES

DR. FRANK FIELD AND JOHN MORSE

RANDOM HOUSE NEW YORK

Copyright © 1992 by Dr. Frank Field

All rights reserved under International and Pan-American Copyright Conventions. Published in the United States by Random House, Inc., New York, and simultaneously in Canada by Random House of Canada Limited, Toronto.

All National Fire Incidents Reporting System illustrations are from *Fire in the United States*, 7th edition, 1983–87, with highlights for 1988.

LIBRARY OF CONGRESS CATALOGING-IN-PUBLICATION DATA
Field, Frank, 1927–
[Get out alive]
Dr. Frank Field's get out alive : save your family's life with
fire survival techniques / by Frank Field and John Morse.
p. cm.
Includes index.
ISBN 0-679-73760-X
1. Fire prevention—Popular works. 2. Fires—Popular works.
I. Morse, John. II. Title.
TH9148.F46 1992
628.9'2—dc20 92-14793
CIP

Manufactured in the United States of America

Book Design by Beth Tondreau Design

Figures 6-1, 6-2, 11-3, 11-4, 11-5, 12-2 and Appendix map
by Harry Chester Associates

First Edition

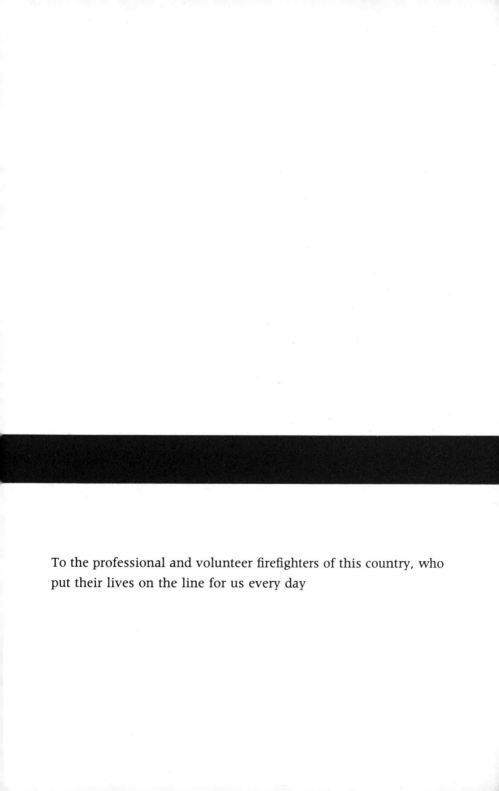

To the professional and volunteer firefighters of this country, who put their lives on the line for us every day

CONTENTS

AUTHORS' NOTE

The information and recommendations in this book have been compiled from what we believe are the best available resources. They represent the most current information on the subject. No warranty, guarantee, endorsement, or representation is made by this book beyond the information presented. We do not exclude the requirement that other information may be necessary under particular circumstances or conditions and assume no responsibility for the completeness or sufficiency of the information contained herein. Rather than place too much value on any single statistic in our book, readers are encouraged to listen to our broader—and more urgent—message of fire safety.

FOREWORD

With the advent of the smoke detector and increased public awareness about the importance of fire safety, residential deaths due to fire have been dramatically reduced during the last two decades.

The more you know about fire prevention and detection, how to safeguard your family and home from fire, and what to do to safely escape a fire, the better your chances for survival if fire tragically strikes.

Fire is a fact of life that has the potential to affect every American. Even more alarming, the United States has one of the highest fire death rates in the world, exceeding all of Western Europe and Asia, despite our nation's superior network of career and volunteer fire departments.

Part of the problem is that many people have serious misconceptions about fire. The purpose of this book is to clear up these faulty assumptions, provide you with the *right* answers about what to do and not to do in a fire, and inform you about how fires can be detected and prevented from starting in the first place.

The United States Fire Administration (USFA) has undertaken a number of major fire safety initiatives to prevent senseless fire tragedies. Working with corporations and other concerned organizations has been a crucial part of this effort. These public-private partnerships provide the resources which enable the USFA to build bridges of lifesaving knowledge with local communities.

To create a more realistic view of what happens in a fire and to encourage Americans to practice home escape plans, the USFA teamed with BRK Electronics, makers of First Alert safety products, McDonald's, and WCBS-TV to develop a consumer education program entitled "Plan to Get Out Alive." This program, including a nationally acclaimed video narrated by Dr. Frank Field and millions of fire safety brochures distributed through McDonald's restaurants throughout the country, has been credited with saving more than 70 lives. "Plan to Get Out Alive" serves as one example of the positive impact public education plays in reducing fire deaths. More important, it demonstrates the role partnerships with private industry play in communicating fire safety messages to the public.

I recommend this book highly to anyone who has a desire to learn how to protect themselves and their families from fire. Preparedness is the key to fire safety, and knowing how to separate the fire "myths" from reality could mean the difference between life and death.

OLIN L. GREENE, ADMINISTRATOR
UNITED STATES FIRE ADMINISTRATION

ACKNOWLEDGMENTS

When the United States Fire Administration, First Alert, McDonald's, and WCBS-TV got together to create the "Plan to Get Out Alive" news series and video, it showed how cooperation among groups and organizations can result in a powerful fire prevention program that saves lives. In writing this book, many individuals and organizations have also generously supplied the facts, figures, support, and expertise to bring the message of fire prevention to even more people. We'd particularly like to thank Fire Administrator Olin Greene, Deputy Administrator Edward

Wall, and Kenneth Kuntz of the United States Fire Administration for their cooperation and thoughtful insight; Philip Schaenman of TriData Corporation for sharing his in-depth knowledge of fire prevention; Gerald Carrino and Richard F. Timmons and all the other people at First Alert for providing the latest information on all phases of fire warning and fire suppression equipment; and Win Baker, for his years of help as a writer and researcher on fire safety.

We'd also like to thank Betsy Nolan, Brice Hammack, Donald Lehr, Ellen Lichtenstein, Judy Johnson, and Carole Cook; and Loretta L. Worters, of the Insurance Information Institute.

Thanks also to Frank Gribbin, New York City Fire Department; Col. H. Lewis Young and Lt. Jim Mykytyn, Cobb County Fire and Emergency Services; Lt. Kevin Baum, Austin, Texas, Fire Department; Assistant Fire Chief James D. Spiegel, Countryside Fire Protection District, Illinois; James Hussey, Arson Prevention Project, Portland, Oregon; Larry Mackler, American Red Cross of Greater New York; Andrew Steinmuller, Nassau County Fire Commission; and U.S. Representative Curt Weldon.

The following organizations and agencies provided invaluable information and assistance: Eastern Paralyzed Veterans Association, National Highway Transportation and Safety Administration, New York Department of State Office of Fire Prevention and Control, New Jersey Bureau of Fire Safety, U.S. Consumer Product Safety Commission, National Fire Sprinkler Association, Children's Television Workshop, U.S. Fire Administration, and TriData Corporation.

INTRODUCTION

It was as though I was staging my own murder.

There I was in the middle of a fire, an inferno purposely set to give a "Learn Not to Burn" news series a bit of television drama. But, with cameras rolling and microphone on, what started out to be a colorful backdrop was suddenly a matter of life and death—*my* life and death.

It began as just another assignment. As Senior Health and Science Editor of WCBS-TV, a station serving almost seven million households in the New York City metropolitan area, I was used to doing whatever it took to enliven the visuals. When it came time to do a series on surviving a fire, I repressed a yawn ("Are 'fire safety' the world's two most boring words?" I wondered) and decided to create some good footage for what I expected to be another rehashed stop-drop-and-roll saw.

The idea of doing on-camera remarks inside an actual fire seemed easy enough. I'd be inside a room used by the New York City Fire Department to study fires and train the men and women known as the city's "Bravest." Several firefighters would be standing nearby. My cameraman would be there. I'd be covered head to toe with insulated, fireproof clothing. I'd be carrying my own oxygen tank. I planned a four-sentence monologue.

My lines were memorized, the camera was in place, ready to roll. Just another assignment.

With cameras rolling, the fire was ignited and I began:

"I never really understood that fires are black and not light."

The heat was almost immediately searing. And the smoke was building much faster than I expected. In the first 10 seconds, my head filled with disastrous scenarios that until then had never even occurred to me. The incredible heat fueled my fear. My only clear thought was that it was time to get out, but I continued:

"That's because until recently I had never experienced what it's like to be in a real fire."

In fact, it wasn't until that moment that I began to understand. My words suddenly seemed self-mocking. The fire puffed billowing smoke into the room, much more with each passing second, and my vision rapidly dimmed in the black cloud. I went on with my lines as the smoke expanded with increasing furor.

"Those of you out there who have been in a fire know what I mean. Most of you don't."

All light totally disappeared in an inky wash of choking air. I lost sight of the firefighters who were standing off-camera. My cameraman standing less than five feet away disappeared, then the camera itself. When I looked down at my hand I couldn't see it.

My mind was racing. "I've done this to myself! I put myself in the middle of a raging fire just to make good television!" I realized: My God! I could die!

My heart pumped furiously. Inside my oxygen mask, my exaggerated breathing sounded like each inhalation would be my last. I felt faint, and in my disorientation, I began to panic. I later learned the temperature at head level was 600° F—hot enough to cook your lungs.

The fire had been burning less than 30 seconds.

Thanks to the cooler heads of the fire professionals, I was pulled from what looked to be certain death.

After it was over, I pondered a revelation that all too often people don't have an opportunity to consider: Until I was caught in a burning room, I had no idea what a fire was really like.

Here I was, a college-educated professional living and working in New York City, a father and a grandfather. My 31 years in television news had given me familiarity with a broad range of subjects. But, all my experience and all my education never prepared me for the deadly realities of fire—an ignorance that could have cost me my life.

As I continued working on the series, researching the gruesome statistics, hearing the horror stories, realizing the immensity of tragedies that are usually preventable, I found myself more and more deeply involved in my seemingly simple assignment.

Why do house fires kill more American children than any disease? Why does Baltimore suffer 13 times as many fire deaths as Amsterdam, a city of similar size? Why do we never take this subject seriously until there's a tragedy on the scale of the 1980 MGM Grand Hotel fire in Las Vegas or the 1984 New Year's Eve disaster at the Dupont Plaza Hotel in San Juan—only to forget within days? Why do cities budget so much money to put out fires and so little money to prevent them?

Unlike any other subject I had ever investigated, this became a story with too many uncomfortable questions to ignore. And every moment I worked on this story I kept remembering my own horrifying experience.

What followed became one of the most intensely researched stories of my news career. I interviewed fire officials from New York to Los Angeles. I prowled burned-out buildings from ghetto neighborhoods to middle-class communities. I went on fire calls where firefighters put their lives on the line for people caught in tragedies that could have been prevented. I heard the chilling stories of fire survivors, some so scarred by burns they asked to be interviewed off-camera.

When my work was done and the final tapes were being edited, I wondered if the effort would be worth it. Would it make any difference? Would anyone want to hear about a subject that even I had found boring at first?

It didn't take long before I knew the answer. ''Plan to Get Out Alive'' set new ratings records at the station for a news segment. And each evening of its three-night broadcast saw an increase in viewers. On the final night, the show's ratings beat prime-time national network competition, a rare feat for a locally produced news show.

Calls and letters poured in from all over the viewing region. Fire chiefs from New York City—home of the world's largest fire department—to small towns where the department is a dozen volunteers described the series as ''lifesaving.'' Twenty-two fire departments subsequently bestowed upon me awards of merit in thanks for my work. They occupy an entire wall of my television office.

Probably my proudest achievement came a few weeks after my ''Plan to Get Out Alive'' series had aired. Karen, a brave little nine-year-old, had seen the series. Weeks later, fire struck her home and Karen became a hero. Karen later told firefighters how she acted single-handedly to save her family. She explained her knowledge of fire's darkness, her awareness of the dangers of breathing smoke. She told how she knew that the fire's fumes were putting her parents into a deeper sleep and that she needed to awaken them. She had watched the series, she said, and what she had learned saved her family's life.

As I present this book, just as when I presented my series, my hope is that at least one person will be spared the terror and tragedy of death or injury by fire. If that goal seems small, consider that you may be that person.

FRANK FIELD
NEW YORK CITY, 1992

DR. FRANK FIELD'S GET OUT ALIVE

1

Learning to Burn

The United States is dead last among industrialized nations in terms of fire damage and loss of life. That is a pathetic record. We need to educate every American—from the very young to the elderly and disabled—about fire safety. We must also reach our government, from the U.S. Congress to the local town council, to give our firefighters the tools to do the job.

—CONGRESSMAN CURT WELDON (R-PA)
CHAIRMAN OF THE CONGRESSIONAL FIRE SERVICES CAUCUS

When it comes to fire, Americans seem to have a death wish.

The United States has one of the highest death rates from fire in the world, 50 percent higher than in most Western European countries. Compared to Austria, the Netherlands, and Switzerland, the rate of fire deaths is three times greater.

Every year, nearly 6,000 Americans die in fires. Although that figure represents a slight decline over the past 10 years, it's still pitifully high. In any given year, more than 20 times more Americans are injured and killed in fires than in tornados, earthquakes, floods, and hurricanes combined.

Of the 200,000 to 300,000 people injured in fires every year, many are scarred and maimed for life. And many who survive the smoke and flames continue to suffer traumatic emotional disturbances. The emotional toll can be devastating. About 100,000 Americans lose their homes to fire each year, along with their treasured possessions, irreplaceable mementos, family photographs, and other precious items. In addition, nearly 40,000 pets are killed in fires annually. People who lose their homes to fire suffer one of the most painful and depressing events of their lives.

Fires in all residences account for about 80 percent of fire deaths and injuries. Over half the victims are under 13 years old.

Before the year is over, about 2.1 million fires will be reported. The direct dollar cost of the destruction will be around $8 billion. The indirect costs, including those attributed to fire departments, insurance, and other costs, will bring the total close to $30 billion. If loss of productivity from deaths and injuries is added, the estimates run as high as $120 billion. In major fires, the lawsuits can run as high as two or three billion dollars.

Every year, more than 100 firefighters are killed and over 60,000 are injured.

AN INTERNATIONAL PERSPECTIVE

If the enormity of the problem is still difficult to grasp, a world perspective may help: Baltimore's death rate from fires is about *13 times* greater than that of Amsterdam, a city approximately the same size. Chicago's population is half the size of Hong Kong's, but it has three times more deaths from fire. As Table 1-1 shows, the United States has one of the highest rates of fire deaths among the industrialized nations of the world.

Why should the United States suffer such extraordinary fire losses? An examination of other countries' attitudes toward fire may help to explain this phenomenon.

Let's begin with Japan, a highly urbanized nation with densely populated cities. Japan stresses fire prevention, reaching out to a large portion of the population repeatedly from preschool through adulthood. With over 100 million people, the entire nation of Japan has fewer fire calls per year than New York City, population about 7.3 million. Japan's low death rate can probably be traced to the Japanese attitude toward fire.

Table 1-1.
DEATHS PER MILLION BY COUNTRY

High (19–33 deaths)	Medium (11–18 deaths)		Low (less than 11 deaths)
South Africa	Sweden	Belgium	West Germany
Hungary	Norway	Japan	Austria
Canada	Britain	France	South Korea
United States	Ireland	Denmark	Netherlands
Finland	New Zealand	Spain	Switzerland
	Hong Kong	Australia	

Source: TriData Corporation

In Japan, a family whose house catches on fire is considered to have brought great dishonor to the neighborhood. Because of the fragile nature of the materials used in most Japanese home construction—typically light wood—any fire represents a danger of immense proportions. For many Japanese, fire is viewed as a personal disgrace rather than an unfortunate accident. Once the fire has been extinguished, a sound truck is sometimes dispatched to the neighborhood to broadcast to neighbors the fact that a nearby homeowner has been careless with fire. Instead of being pitied, the homeowners can expect to be ostracized as thoughtless neighbors who endangered everyone around them. Those unlucky enough to have had even a small house fire are usually shunned for their carelessness. Often the ostracism is so severe, the family is forced to move away from the neighborhood.

As might be expected, Japan also has a strict attitude about fire prevention. Fire professionals and the volunteers who assist them visit virtually every residence in many parts of the country at least once a year to ensure fire code compliance. Children in most cities usually get an intensive fire safety education in school by the time they are 12. After that, refresher courses are given annually. A student's normal day may be as likely to include a fire safety drill as courses in such academic subjects as mathematics and science. From preschool children to workers on the job, the population is bombarded with fire safety messages.

But that's Japan, you say, a country where discipline and outside control are more culturally accepted. But Japan is not alone in its vigilance. The attitudes of nations around the world toward fire

 Six thousand Americans die every year in fires.

prevention are similar to Japan's. It is the United States that stands out for its deadly, casual fire policy.

Let's look at Australia, a nation much closer to the American model. Here a chief fire warden is appointed to each multistory building, public or private, with an individual fire warden for each floor. During the dry season, November through April, fire danger notices are broadcast daily. On "ban days" it is illegal to start outside fires, even barbecues.

In England, the government spends millions of dollars annually to have professionals develop effective fire prevention advertising campaigns. The ads are not run in competition with other public service announcements on late-night television; instead, the government buys air time during prime-time programs to reach the largest audience. The government also purchases time during daytime soap operas. Not only does the message reach the general populace, it also gets to low-income viewers (who constitute a significant audience share of daytime dramas), a group that suffers an extraordinary percentage of fire deaths and injuries. On average, the United Kingdom spends eight times more per capita on the national level for fire prevention than the United States.

In Germany and Sweden, every home's chimney is inspected from one to four times a year. In Switzerland, in an effort to preserve the character of the cities (which also serves to deter arson), insurance companies pay damages only if buildings destroyed by fire are rebuilt on the same spot. In France, it is common insurance practice for building owners to take at least a partial loss. In some countries, insurance companies refuse to allow an owner to insure a building for 100 percent of its value. And in other countries, the owner must pay a fine if found negligent. In the Netherlands, where nearly everyone watches the 8 P.M. news on TV, fire prevention messages regularly accompany the broadcast. The fire death rate in the Netherlands at the end of the

1980s was 6.2 per million; by contrast, the U.S. rate was 24.2 per million.

OUR DEADLY ATTITUDE

The trend over the past decade for our national fire prevention effort has been to cut the budget, sometimes so severely that the U.S. Fire Administration nearly disappeared entirely.

Our own memories of giggle-filled school fire drills are telling of the American attitude toward fires. Fire drills serve a purpose, we feel, but for other people, not us. Fires themselves are something that happens to other people, not to us. Even when a tragedy occurs in our own city or town—even in our own neighborhood—most of us consider it a matter of bad luck for the individuals involved, but it has nothing to do with us.

When someone we know becomes the victim of a fire, the first question (after "Did anybody get hurt?") is, "Do you have insurance?" In many countries, the response would be, "How could you let it happen?"

However, it wasn't always that way. As far back as the 1600s, when the Dutch governor of New Amsterdam (later New York City) first authorized a fire department, the city imposed a penalty of three shillings on owners whose buildings caught fire due to defective flues and fireplaces. If the owner had already been warned about fire safety, the fine increased to 40 shillings.

Today our public information campaigns are often dull, boring, forgettable, and wishy-washy. Edward Wall, deputy administrator

 Between 200,000 and 300,000 Americans are injured in fires every year.

for the U.S. Fire Administration, says, "Community educators like to talk to the Sunnyvales of the world. They want a happy message. But when you're dealing with adults—well, if you don't smack it really hard, the message isn't heard. They only listen if you get their attention." Think about it: Can you remember the last fire safety message you saw on television, heard on the radio, or read in a newspaper?

The U.S. Fire Administration, a division of the Federal Emergency Management Agency (FEMA), has made some inroads. Their "Let's Retire Fire" campaign targets older Americans, a group that suffers an inordinate percentage of fire deaths. In a coalition with Safe Kids, the organization that spearheaded the bicycle helmet safety campaign, the U.S. Fire Administration has developed more than 65 local programs to teach children about fire safety. It has solicited the aid of Fortune 500 companies to join in a cooperative information effort. Another campaign teamed up with McDonald's, a company that has used its many restaurants to reach the public directly with fire safety messages through such innovations as providing fire safety tips on serving-tray liners.

But, while some federal agencies thrive, the U.S. Fire Administration has often had to struggle over the past decade with relatively minuscule annual budgets—between 8 and 24 million dollars. Thus, the entire federal budget for fire prevention for over 250 million Americans amounts to less than 10 cents per person per year.

As a result, our awareness of fire safety is extremely low. As Edward Wall says, "If you ask someone to tell you what hazards their family faces, they'll tell you crime, car accidents, anything but fires. Fire is way down on that list."

Philip Schaenman, formerly of the U.S. Fire Administration and currently president of TriData Corporation, one of the nation's leading fire research organizations, argues that as a nation we have the know-how to prevent the majority of fires. "The fact that we don't," he says, "is shocking."

Americans, says Wall, don't like discipline and they don't like people intruding.

It's all part of an attitude that's killing us.

THE PREVENTABLE TRAGEDY

If any single thing has helped lower the U.S. fire death rate, it's the smoke detector. But even though about 85 percent of American homes have a smoke detector, so lackadaisical is our attitude that one-tenth to one-third of smoke detectors are useless because of dead or missing batteries or vandalism. Experts estimate that in most cases where people died by fire in homes equipped with smoke detectors, the detector didn't work. Firefighters often tell of discovering victims who appear to be asleep, covered by a thin layer of soot. Because there was no alarm to wake them, they were killed, probably within the first five minutes of the outbreak of the fire, by fumes that lulled them into a deeper sleep.

Most fires, fire deaths, and fire injuries are preventable. The U.S. Fire Administration estimates that as many as eight of 10 fires could be prevented. But most of us choose to ignore that simple fact. Few people comprehend the fatal power of fires.

The carelessness with which many teenagers view the destructive power of fire is typical of the problem. Some of them, particu-

 A fire is black. You won't be able to see in a fire.

larly young males, like to fool around with gasoline. Few of these kids understand that gasoline can explode like a bomb.

The approach that adults take to fire safety is not much wiser.

No thinking person would leave a loaded gun within reach of a child, but how many parents make a conscious effort to keep lighters and matches out of the reach of children? Curious children are a prime cause of fires. A New York fire marshal once told me that a cigarette lighter is more deadly in the hands of a child than most parents ever realize—until it's too late. And children don't know the potential of matches and lighters to injure or kill. Ask your children where the matches in the house are kept. Don't be surprised if they know exactly where to find them.

The public has clamored for laws that would punish drunk drivers as criminals. But if an intoxicated person happens to make it home without a wreck, then lights a cigarette and falls asleep, starting a fire that kills others, it does not occur to us that the resulting fire is a criminal act.

Although we consider crime prevention a subject worthy of study by universities, think tanks, and congressional committees, fire prevention gets short shrift. The media have not helped. Think of all the times you've read compilations of crime statistics. How many murders per city, per year. Robberies, burglaries, rapes . . . the press can't get enough. But how often have you seen statistics on deaths and injuries due to fires? Have you ever seen an annual roundup? a city-by-city breakdown? a 10-year trend?

 The biggest mistake you can make in a fire is to panic. The best way to prevent panic is to prepare.

Think of other deadly disasters. When a killer hurricane rips through a city and leaves four dead, it's covered by all the national newsweeklies. An earthquake that kills one person becomes the lead story on the network news. But when a fire snuffs out the life of a mother and her children, the story merits only a few inches of type in the local news and is forgotten before the next day's edition.

Even on the front line of fire safety, in the fire halls across the country, a miniscule portion of the budget is devoted to fire safety education. Most fire departments allocate three percent of their budgets to education, 97 percent to suppression.

Unquestionably that 97 percent has paid off. No nation knows how to put out a fire better or faster than the United States. But our exemplary efforts are too often at the expense of preventing the tragedy in the first place.

TriData's Philip Schaenman points out that up to 10 percent of the budgets of many fire departments in foreign nations is spent on prevention. According to Schaenman, if fire departments in our country would shift only one percent of their budgets from suppression to prevention, although the change for the suppression budget would be negligible, it would represent as much as a 30 to 50 percent increase for prevention.

So why don't they do it? "Local politicians want to see that big red fire truck parked in their district," says the U.S. Fire Administration's Edward Wall—a reflection of the emphasis on suppression over prevention.

A recent TriData survey of the nation's mayors indicated that

 Chances are you will experience three serious fires during your lifetime.

while most of them rate fire education as the number one way to prevent fires, at least one-third of the cities had no full-time public education personnel. Most cities with fire education departments have a maximum of three persons in that department, *regardless of the city's size or its incidence of death from fires.*

Fire departments often find that even when they have volunteers at their disposal, paying for educational materials is still out of the question. As recently as the 1980s, San Francisco and Los Angeles allocated almost no money for fire prevention materials. Both cities relied on donations. Can you imagine their police departments having to beg for donations to do their jobs?

New York City, with the oldest and largest fire department in the United States has only 12 employees who work full-time in fire safety education—a total of 12 out of a work force of over 13,600 to reach nearly eight million people. Philip Schaenman tells of one New York battalion chief who complained, "I can get 50 engine companies to come to my district if I need them, but I cannot borrow a copy of *Countdown to Disaster* [an educational film sponsored by the National Fire Prevention Association]."

Compare the American attitude toward prevention with that of Japanese officials. In Osaka, Japan, all of the regular firefighters are given desks, so that when they're not extinguishing fires, they can handle the paperwork involved in fire safety education, which they view as a tool for fire protection that is as important as an axe or a hose.

The situation in American schools is no better than in city halls, even though children constitute the majority of fire fatalities. For one thing, the teachers already feel overburdened by other educational tasks. Those who do decide to instruct their students find that most fire safety education material is outdated and boring. In addition, the materials are often too expensive to fit into an already strained school budget. In most schools, funds for fire education are almost nonexistent. In many big city school budgets, millions are allocated for driver education, zero for fire prevention. Yet high school students and young adults have the highest fire injury rate of any age group.

Communities across the country have proven again and again that fire prevention programs work, that they save lives and they save money. After the rural community of Seaside on the Oregon coast instituted a fire safety program, the incidence of home fires dropped by 61 percent in this town of 5,000. In Waterford, Connecticut, a fire prevention program was introduced into the public school system, and students were asked to pass the information along to their families. Within two years, the incidence of chimney, structure, and outdoor fires was cut in half (Figure 1-1).

In suburban Atlanta, when Fire Chief David Hilton decided to reorganize the Cobb County fire department in 1976, he increased his expenditures for fire prevention to 10 percent of the overall budget. A landmark sprinkler law was enacted which included a voluntary sprinkler program for single-family homes; the law encourages sprinkler installation during construction by offering economic trade-offs, such as reduced fire retardant ratings for walls. A safety education program was introduced in the schools. By 1990, the county's population was 450,800, more than double that of 1976. Using trends established before the prevention program was in place, 7,663 fires were projected for 1990. Instead, only 1,468

 Typically, children who die as a result of playing with matches are around three years old.

Figure 1-1.

WATERFORD, CONNECTICUT:
FIRE PREVENTION PROGRAM RESULTS

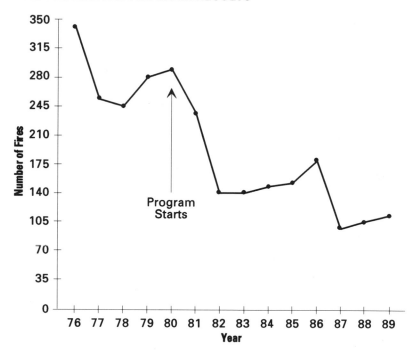

Note: This graph represents the combined number of structure, chimney, and outdoor fires. Vehicle fires have not been included because they were unlikely to be affected by the public education program.

Source: TriData Corporation

fires were reported. Residential fire deaths fell dramatically. At the same time, homeowners' insurance premiums dropped markedly. (See Chapter 12 for more information.)

WHY DON'T WE DO MORE?

Most communities don't do more probably because they are simply unaware of the fact that most fires are preventable.

Figure 1-2.
FIRE DEATHS IN THE U.S.

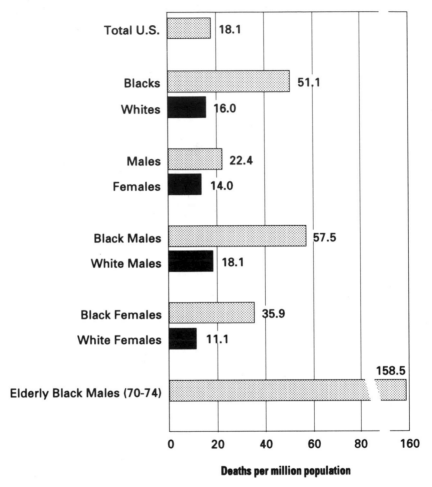

Deaths per million population

Source: National Fire Incidents Reporting System

16

Fire singles out the elderly and the very young; it disproportionately attacks the poor, African-Americans and Native Americans, urban and rural dwellers (Figure 1-2). It is, however, one of the few major social problems for which there are existing technical solutions. But all across our country, every day, people continue to die needlessly by fire.

2

What Happens in a Fire

It hits you like you've been hit by a Mack truck. It's so hot that there's no way to explain it.

—A FIRE SURVIVOR

Most people never dream that they'll be caught in a fire, and until it happens, they have no idea how devastating the power of a fire can be. That's because they have received no practical education on what really happens in a fire.

The fire victim quoted above was lucky—she survived, despite her ignorance. Discovering that her kitchen was on fire, she ran to the phone to dial 911. But the fire spread so quickly that even before she could hang up, she was flattened by a blast of heat and smoke. She was badly burned in the explosion, but because she had been knocked to the floor, she had enough air to survive until the fire department rescued her—four minutes after she made the call.

When I interviewed her for my WCBS-TV fire safety series, months after the fire, only a small part of her face was visible from behind the bandages that covered her head, neck, upper body, and arms and hands. She now knew the dangers of fire, she told me, but she had learned the hard way.

One of the main reasons fire catches so many people by surprise is because of the inaccurate portrayal of fire on television and in the movies. Think about *The Towering Inferno*. Remember the scenes of leaping flames, daring rescues, people running through burning rooms? Director Ron Howard's 1991 movie *Backdraft* was highly praised by firefighters for its gripping drama, even though it perpetuated the old myths, too. Fire is not a stage set for dramatic heroics. Hollywood's version of fire is a lie.

Let's examine the four main features of a fire.

FIRE IS BLACK

The biggest misconception about fire concerns visibility. Fire is black. Considering the intensity of flames, you might think that a room on fire would be filled with light. But fire is not bright. It

 Ninety percent of fire fatalities are due in whole or in part to smoke and gas.

creates so much smoke that within minutes the room turns pitch black. You cannot even see your hand in front of your face.

Even when they have flashlights, firefighters often inspect rooms using the sense of touch to help them find victims hidden by the smoky atmosphere. One survivor described the air as ''blacker than black.'' People who have been in burning buildings will tell you that they had no notion of the profound darkness that would accompany the blaze.

Imagine the sheer terror of being trapped inside a fire. Then imagine how that terror would intensify if you discovered you also couldn't see, that you were literally blinded by the smoke. How would you escape?

In a fire, you will be blind. That's why it's essential that you practice your fire escape route from your bedroom with your eyes closed. If it seems difficult now, you can imagine how frightening the experience would be if it were the real thing: panic, screaming, intense heat, and utter darkness.

SMOKE KILLS

The second thing you must understand about fire is that it's not the flames that will probably kill you, it's the smoke and gas. Fire produces toxic fumes that can kill you with just a few breaths.

One of the most toxic gases created by fires is carbon monoxide. Just like the exhaust from a car, the carbon monoxide in a fire will at first make you dizzy and disoriented, then knock you out, and

 The carbon monoxide created by a fire numbs your brain. It leaves you disoriented and dizzy and eventually kills you.

ultimately kill you. Carbon monoxide is odorless, so don't expect to smell it.

One fire survivor I interviewed told me of waking up to the sound of the smoke detector and getting out of bed. As he walked to his door, he began to feel paralyzed. He could see the door, he knew he wanted to walk to the door, but he couldn't move. He became dizzy and collapsed. His father, who was crawling on the floor, pulled him to safety.

Firefighters often tell of discovering fire victims dead in bed with a thin layer of soot on their faces, looking as though they're sleeping. When a fire breaks out, acrid, noxious smoke fills the room. Most people think that the smell of smoke would wake them. But in fact the carbon monoxide that accompanies the fire often causes you to go into a deeper sleep.

More and more often, wall coverings, countertops, furniture, appliances, toys, apparel, and other household items are made of plastic. When they melt in fires, they can release deadly fumes. Other common household items, such as cleansers, spray paints, and hair spray, can create explosive, toxic brews when exposed to fire. The fumes tend to rise and accumulate at the ceiling, so danger increases at higher levels in the room. Sometimes people are killed in a fire simply because they sit up in bed when they hear the alarm. If you stand up, the smoke at eye level makes it impossible to breath. It is like holding your head under water; you are literally drowning in the fumes. The fumes numb your brain, making it extremely difficult to move your arms and legs. They trap you as surely as if you were in chains.

FIRE IS HOT

The third fact you must learn about fire is that the intensity of the heat alone can kill you. The heat stops your body from functioning.

Heat builds rapidly in a room that's on fire. One of the biggest dangers is known as "flashover." In flashover, the heat becomes so intense that everything in the room catches fire. Even if the fire is confined to one end of the room, everything in the room will burn: furniture, walls, people. Even the smoke in the room will catch on fire.

> The fire that struck the 22-story Dupont Plaza Hotel in San Juan on New Year's Eve in 1986 is a case in point. The 423-room hotel had been booked to capacity. Two disgruntled employees later admitted to starting the fire in a storage room next to a second-floor casino. After building up power, the fire broke into the casino and a rush of oxygen fed the flames. Survivors later reported that they thought a bomb had exploded. There was no bomb, but the impact of the flashover had the same result. Ninety-six people died in that blaze, and one more died a few days later. All but two died in the first few minutes, victims of the casino fireball.
>
> Later, Edward Wall, Deputy Administrator for the U.S. Fire Administration, told reporters, "This is what happens when an ordinary fire starts in a structure with no detectors, no functioning alarms, and no sprinklers." Besides the 97 killed, 140 others were seriously injured.

By the time the temperature reaches 150°F—less than one minute after a fire begins in a room—your body stops functioning. Intense heat causes instant shock. One breath of air that hot will sear your lungs. Soon after, the temperature at head level is a mind-boggling 600°F. At the ceiling, it's 1,000°F—about four

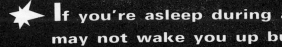

If you're asleep during a fire, the smoke may not wake you up but put you into a deeper sleep instead.

times the temperature of boiling water. That's why firefighters never walk into burning buildings: They crawl. Given these incredible temperatures, you can easily see why all those Hollywood versions of people racing through blazing buildings are patently absurd.

FIRE SPREADS QUICKLY

The fourth fact to know is that you have only seconds to escape. Most of us think that we would have at least a few minutes to get out. But time is against you in a fire. People who step away from a burning room to fill a bucket with water or grab a fire extinguisher often return to find that a small fire has grown into a raging inferno. If they're lucky enough to survive they are likely to tell others that the fire moved so rapidly that they were helpless against it.

A fire that starts in a wastepaper basket can engulf a room in flames in two minutes. The heat is great enough to knock you unconscious. Within three minutes, it would be impossible to survive in the burning room, and the fire would have spread throughout that level of the structure. Within five minutes, an entire two-story house can catch on fire.

An escape plan is critical to get out alive. Chances are you will have no more than three minutes to escape a fire in your home. If it takes two minutes for smoke to trigger the detector, that leaves you with one minute to get out. Could you crawl out of your room, alert everyone in the house, and escape in one minute? That's why you have to plan ahead.

3
Cause and Effect

Although the damage and havoc fire can wreak are clear, the causes of fire are much less obvious. In learning how to prevent fires, it's important to know why and where fires strike. Seventy-four percent of fire deaths and 66 percent of fire injuries occur in private residences (see Figures 3-1 and 3-2), but while hotel and office fires grab the headlines, fire deaths at home often go unnoticed by the media.

Figure 3-1.

FIRE DEATHS BY LOCATION

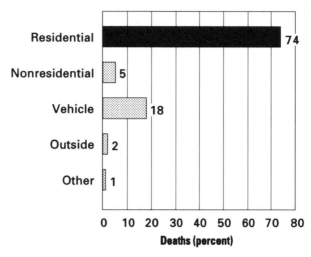

Source: National Fire Incidents Reporting System

Figure 3-2.

FIRE INJURIES BY LOCATION

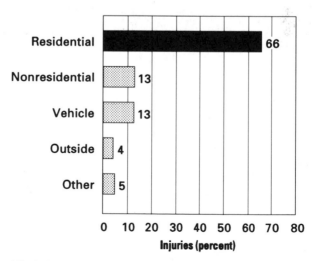

Source: National Fire Incidents Reporting System

CAUSES OF FIRE

Fires are measured in several ways—by fire deaths, fire injuries, dollar loss, and fire incidence. For each of these four categories, there is a different set of causes. The three leading causes of fire deaths in private homes are careless smoking, arson, and heating (Figure 3-3). However, of the three leading causes of residential fires overall, heating ranks number one, cooking accidents is second, and arson ranks third (Figure 3-4).

Figure 3-3.
CAUSES OF RESIDENTIAL FIRE DEATHS

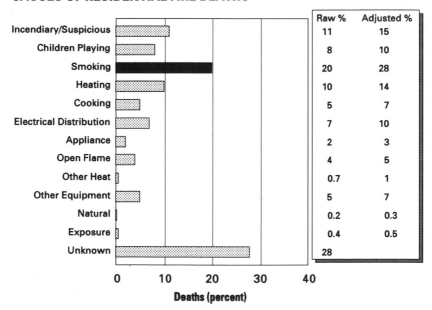

	Raw %	Adjusted %
Incendiary/Suspicious	11	15
Children Playing	8	10
Smoking	20	28
Heating	10	14
Cooking	5	7
Electrical Distribution	7	10
Appliance	2	3
Open Flame	4	5
Other Heat	0.7	1
Other Equipment	5	7
Natural	0.2	0.3
Exposure	0.4	0.5
Unknown	28	

Deaths (percent)

Source: National Fire Incidents Reporting System

Figure 3-4.
CAUSES OF RESIDENTIAL FIRES

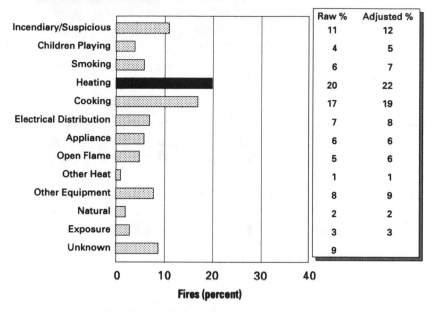

	Raw %	Adjusted %
Incendiary/Suspicious	11	12
Children Playing	4	5
Smoking	6	7
Heating	20	22
Cooking	17	19
Electrical Distribution	7	8
Appliance	6	6
Open Flame	5	6
Other Heat	1	1
Other Equipment	8	9
Natural	2	2
Exposure	3	3
Unknown	9	

Fires (percent)

Source: National Fire Incidents Reporting System

Careless Smoking

Misuse of smoking materials is the leading cause of all residential fire deaths, even though it does not rank as one of the top three causes of residential fires overall (see Figure 3-3). Although many deaths result from smoking in bed, more often, fires that cause death are started as a result of smoking in the lounging areas of the home, such as the living room, den, or playroom. Typically a cigarette falls between the furniture cushions and upholstery—often dropped by someone who has been drinking—where it smolders for hours before bursting into flames. This lapse of time between dropping the cigarette and the actual start of the fire makes it easy to see how a furniture fire can catch victims unawares and lead to death.

In 1991 three Brooklyn teenagers perished in a fire caused by the careless smoking habits of a downstairs neighbor. Despite the deployment of a team of 90 firefighters, the lives of Tony, Penelope, and Donnel were ended by a burning cigarette dropped into a mattress on the floor below their apartment.

That same year English firefighters couldn't save Steve Marriott, the lead musician of the rock group Humble Pie, best known for his recording of "Itchycoo Park." In April 1991 he had just returned to his 16th-century cottage in Essex after a two-week recording session. Marriott had high hopes for a comeback, but his career came to a brutal end in a fire, probably caused by a cigarette left unattended in his bedroom.

Arson

"Arson" is a legal term with a somewhat narrow definition. It's also a term used to describe the broader fire category known as "incendiary and suspicious." Under any name it's deadly.

The 1991 fire at the Happy Land Social Club in New York City was traced to arson. Eighty-seven people died in a matter of minutes, leaving scores of children orphaned and hundreds of lives forever changed, all because one man was seeking revenge against a woman who had rebuffed him.

Julio Gonzalez was later convicted of purposely setting the fire to get back at his ex-girlfriend. Gonzalez told how, after an argument with the woman at the club, he filled a one-gallon plastic container with a dollar's worth of gasoline. He returned to the club and doused the entrance of the crowded dance hall, lit a match, ignited the door, then went home to sleep.

Whether Gonzalez intended to kill everyone isn't important (the ex-girlfriend was one of only a handful of survivors). Scores of people were murdered that night.

Gonzalez's intentions remain murky, but the disgruntled workers who started the San Juan Dupont Plaza Hotel fire later told the FBI and fire inspectors that they hadn't meant to kill anybody, just to cause trouble for their employer. Nevertheless, 97 people died and scores more were injured.

Arson is the third leading cause of residential fires, and it is on the increase. Arson is the number one cause of fire dollar loss. Fraud—usually bilking an insurance company—remains the leading motivation for arson, but many other reasons have been cited, including vandalism, revenge, and quarrels. Fire has become an increasingly popular method for expressing anger.

While major disasters like the Happy Land Social Club and Dupont Plaza Hotel infernos get the attention of the public and underscore the tragedy of arson, it's important to remember that most people who die in arson fires are killed in groups of one, two, or three, and that these crimes are committed every day, every year.

Cooking

Cooking is the number one cause of injuries and the second leading cause of all residential fires. Most kitchen fires can be traced to heat sources that are left unattended while cooking. These accidents could easily be prevented by being more vigilant during meal preparation. In addition, knowing how to use baking soda or a pot lid to extinguish a grease fire (like knowing how to stop, drop, and

 Fire is the third leading cause of accidental deaths in the home.

roll when your clothes catch fire) would help reduce the injury rate associated with cooking fires.

Twenty years ago, cooking fires were the leading cause of all residential fires, but as more and more people have turned to alternative heating systems such as wood stoves and space heaters since the energy crisis of the 1970s, heating has replaced cooking as the cause of most fires.

Heating

Nothing causes more residential fires than heating hazards. The incidence of home fires jumps dramatically during the winter months. Bad wiring, poor ventilation, and dirty exhaust ducts contribute to the problem, but mostly it's misuse of space heaters, fireplaces, central heating systems, and wood-burning stoves that make heating the nation's number one residential fire hazard.

In New York City, a tragic 1989 fire that killed three children and critically injured their parents was traced to a faulty electrical space heater. A fourth child, 13-year-old April, had been testing the heater in various outlets, trying to find one that wouldn't make it shoot sparks. After finding one in the living room, she plugged in the heater and went to bed.

Everyone in the house was asleep when the fire broke out. The two-story home had two smoke detectors, but batteries had been removed from both of them. April had closed her bedroom door, so she managed to escape unharmed. Her mother was admitted to the hospital in critical condition, suffering from severe smoke inhalation. The father received third-degree burns over 56 percent of his body. He had attempted to rescue his youngest child, but ended up throwing himself through a window on the second floor to escape the flames.

One firefighter told the *The New York Times* the next day that he had crawled on his stomach through the thick smoke and the intense heat, trying to save two of the children. "I was going just on the sense of touch. That's when I felt the little girl. She was lying on the floor. I reached up onto the bed next to her and felt the little boy. They were lifeless."

The most recent figures available from the U.S. Fire Administration reveal that one of five residential fires is related to heating. Additionally, one of ten fire deaths results from heating problems. Heating fires are the third leading cause of death and the second leading cause of dollar loss.

The U.S. Consumer Product Safety Commission estimates that in 1988, 140 Americans died as a result of portable heaters. The fires caused $43 million in property damage.

This critical component of the residential fire problem includes fireplaces, portable space heaters, wood stoves, water heaters, fixed room heaters, and central heating. Because centralized heating systems in apartment complexes are normally subject to regular professional maintenance, heating is the cause of only about seven percent of fires in this type of residence. Most fires occur in one- and two-family homes. Of all the non–central heating fires, 75 percent are caused by human error, such as faulty installation. Even the most safely designed unit can be a hazard.

The tragedies surrounding heating fires are rife with preventable mistakes. Their victims are of all ages, but the very young and the very old are at greatest risk. Preventing these horrors requires con-

 Fires kill more Americans every year than all natural emergencies combined, including floods, hurricanes, tornados, and earthquakes.

stant vigilance and extreme caution with any kind of heating system, particularly freestanding heaters.

Besides the burns that result from touching these devices, there is also the danger that nearby materials could catch on fire, such as furniture, walls, curtains, carpet, and clothing. And there is grave danger in the smoke and gases heaters often create.

WOOD-BURNING STOVES

When the old-fashioned wood-burning stove became a popular solution to the energy crisis in the 1970s, it brought with it a resurgence of old problems that more modern systems had eliminated. Between 1980 and 1984, Oregon alone recorded 7,000 wood stove fires that caused 32 deaths. Improper installation, ill-fitting vents and pipes, malfunctioning flues, and chimney-related problems all made a vigorous comeback as fire hazards.

Therefore, if you use a wood-burning stove, be sure that it has been properly installed and is well maintained. Three of four wood-burning stove fires are related to improper installation. Each fall, the stove should be inspected (by you, if you know what you're doing, or, if not, by a professional) for cracks in the lining or other defects. Hairline cracks can allow heat leaks that expose surrounding surfaces to temperatures equivalent to a blowtorch.

When installing the stove in your home, be sure that it is kept at least one yard away from anything flammable and that the exhaust pipe is at least 18 inches from the wall. Only one stove should be used per exhaust pipe. The stove should be set at least four inches above the floor on a fire-resistant base such as bricks or a stone slab.

 Over 100,000 homes are lost to fire every year in the United States.

Never place a wood stove in front of a window or door that serves as a fire exit. Always keep a fire extinguisher nearby.

Exhaust pipes should never have severe bends; a 45° angle is optimal. Pipe should be secured with at least three screws at each connection, and furnace cement should be used to seal joints.

When choosing fuel, use only seasoned wood, never green. Hickory and oak burn best. Seasoned wood is wood that has the moisture removed. Because it is drier, it provides far more heat than green wood. To ensure that it is dry, look for wood that has peeling bark and is lighter in color. When two pieces of seasoned wood are hit together, they make a "cracking" noise, as opposed to a dull thud.

Not only does green wood create a low fire that smolders and gives off less heat, it also produces excess creosote. Creosote lines the chimney, creating a fire hazard. Creosote is highly flammable. Whether in the form of a liquid, a shiny glaze, or dry flakes, creosote is dark brown or black and usually gives off a strong, unpleasant odor.

To combat creosote buildup, make a small, intensely hot fire in the stove and stoke it for 15 to 30 minutes each day to eliminate the buildup from the day before. The temperature gauge on the outside of the stove should reach between 500° and 600°F. After a good burn, the fire can be reduced to about 350°F.

Never use trash, charcoal, liquid fuels such as gasoline or kerosene, or artificial logs in the stove. These substances can emit

 The death rate from fires in the United States is 50 percent higher than that of most other industrialized nations, 100–200 percent higher than many.

dangerous gases. The liquid fuels, in particular, could lead to disastrous fires.

Regardless of how well the stove is maintained on a daily basis, the stove and chimney should be professionally cleaned at least once a year, preferably before winter begins.

CHIMNEYS

Chimneys are the lungs of a fuel-burning system. If they have leaks and cracks, or if they are too small, plugged up, or clogged with soot and creosote, they can shut down the respiratory system of the heater, just as an injury can collapse your lungs.

When you decide to use a fuel-burning heater in your home, you should first consider whether or not your chimney is up to the job. Just because a heating system provides you with lots of warmth, that doesn't mean that it won't rob the air of oxygen.

Two teenage boys in Minnesota recently paid the ultimate price for not understanding the need for adequate ventilation. Even though they had opened a window in their tiny cabin, it wasn't enough to ventilate their wood-burning stove. While they slept soundly in their cozy, warm cabin, the stove used up all the oxygen in the air. Both boys suffocated.

Every year, millions of new fireplaces and stoves are installed in the United States. The popularity of this type of heating system has led to a parallel growth in carbon monoxide deaths due to improperly ventilated heating systems. Each year, about 400 Americans die from carbon monoxide poisoning due to faulty home heating systems.

Carbon monoxide is an insidious poison, a colorless, odorless gas that lulls its victims into a deep sleep that ends in death. It catches its victims unaware, leaving them disoriented and groggy. Survivors describe its effect as debilitating, something akin to being paralyzed.

Carbon monoxide killed six Cape Cod campers in early 1991. After bringing a heater into their tent, two adults and four children suffocated because the well-sealed tent kept out the cold, but it also kept out a fresh supply of oxygen.

Chimneys that exhaust smoke to the outdoors should never be any smaller than the pipe leading from the stove or heater. The flue should always be large enough for the pipe. Variance leading to poor ventilation is a health threat.

Begin by inspecting the outside of your chimney visually. Do you notice any creosote bleeding through the mortar lining? (It will resemble dark streaks of paint.) Is the chimney deteriorating in any way? Is mortar breaking away from the bricks? Are the bricks between the chimney and the roofline loose? Are bricks cracked, especially at offsets, the places where the bricks on the next row meet? Is the brick mortar hard, or would a sharp object easily pierce it? Does flashing—protective metal plates—surround the chimney and separate it at least two inches from roof shingles? Do you see any blistering of paint at any point where the chimney is behind a wall?

Signs such as these indicate a tear in the chimney lining that could lead to a heat leak, exposing the roof and interior of the house to extremely high temperatures and posing a fire risk. The flue, which regulates the air between the burning fuel and the chimney, should also be cleaned regularly to prevent soot and creosote buildup.

 Annually, 40,000 Americans suffer traumatic emotional disturbances as a result of a fire.

KEROSENE HEATERS

Heating a home with a kerosene heater can be extremely risky. Manufacturers of kerosene heaters rightly claim that there is no danger when they are used properly. The problem is that they are so often mishandled. The number of deaths attributable to kerosene heaters in some areas has been so high, in fact, that many communities and some states have banned their use. As Frank Martinez of the New York City Fire Department once told me, by banning the use of kerosene heaters in 1955, New York eliminated the potential danger. The fire death rate from these devices in New York City dropped from 189 fatalities in the 10 years before the ban to 31 in the 10 years after the ban.

However, some areas still sell kerosene heaters even though they've been banned. Therefore, even if kerosene stoves are sold in your area, don't assume it is legal to use them. Check with your local fire department to be sure.

The consequences of using a kerosene heater can be disastrous:

> When José R. and his 14-year-old son tried to light a kerosene heater in a van parked outside their Brooklyn apartment building, the stove exploded like a bomb. José had used gasoline instead of kerosene, a deadly—but all too common—error. José was found unconscious at the back of the van. His son died with his arm piercing the van's back window.

If you must use a kerosene heater, never use gasoline. Gasoline can explode. Use only 1-K grade clear kerosene. Kerosene should be purchased fresh each winter. Refueling should always be done outdoors. A heater should be totally cooled before refueling, otherwise a fire could ignite when the kerosene touches the heater. Actually, the result is closer to an explosion.

Limit the amount of kerosene you keep in storage to five gallons, and be sure it is in an airtight container designed to hold this type of fuel. Kerosene is poison. It should always be stored carefully so that children will not be exposed to it. Never top off the fuel. Like gasoline, kerosene can expand and pour out of the top of the tank.

As with other types of heaters, be sure that the room is well ventilated. Ironically, it is the homes that are best insulated that represent the greatest danger in terms of ventilation, because they are so well sealed. Always turn off the heater when you leave the room. Never leave a kerosene heater on while you are sleeping.

When Consumers Union, the publisher of *Consumer Reports,* tested kerosene heaters in 1982, it found that they gave off a lot more than heat, including gases such as carbon monoxide, carbon dioxide, sulfur dioxide, and nitrogen dioxide. These poisons were at levels high enough to present a serious health hazard to pregnant women, children, the elderly, asthmatics, or anyone with a respiratory ailment. The levels of some gases were high enough to pose a risk for anyone. When the organization did an update in 1985, it found some improvement, but it still described the new heaters as "worrisome."

Even though manufacturers have gone a long way toward making their products safer, I personally recommend that you avoid kerosene stoves. Suitable alternatives exist that can provide heat with peace of mind and in accordance with all local ordinances.

ELECTRICAL HEATERS

Electrical space heaters offer a relatively safe heating alternative, but like any heating device, they must be handled with extreme caution. Every year, improperly handled electrical heaters cause

Fires cause a direct loss of over $8 billion annually in the United States.

deaths, injuries, and hundreds of millions of dollars in property losses.

Whenever using space heaters of any type, keep all flammable materials at least three feet away. Direct contact with the heating element can cause burns. Check the heater regularly for cracked or frayed wires. Make sure that there is an automatic turnoff switch in case the heater accidentally tips over. The automatic turnoff switch should also work when the unit overheats.

Watch for overloaded wiring when using electrical space heaters. Overloaded wiring causes fires by overheating cords.

When purchasing space heaters, always look for the UL (Underwriters Laboratories) symbol, a sign that the unit has been approved by an independent testing agency.

Children Playing with Fire

Children who play with matches are the source of one of the most tragic fire statistics. Playing with fire increased rapidly in the 1980s as a cause of fires and fire injuries; it now ranks as the third leading cause of fire injuries. Furthermore, children playing with fire constitutes the fourth leading cause of residential fire deaths (see Chapter 4).

Similarly, playing with open flames—a category that includes candles, matches, lighters, embers, ashes, sparks, and torches—

 Costs related to fires—including insurance payments, medical treatment, productivity losses, prevention programs and suppression—exceed $120 billion annually in the United States.

represents the third leading cause of dollar loss in residential fires. This is a growing cause of fires in the category of residential fire deaths and injuries.

WHEN FIRES OCCUR

Fire is not random and neither is the time of day that it strikes. Over the years, emerging trends have shown that the majority of fires and fire deaths occur at distinct times of the days (see Figures 3-5 and 3-6).

Figure 3-5.
RESIDENTIAL FIRE DEATHS BY TIME OF DAY

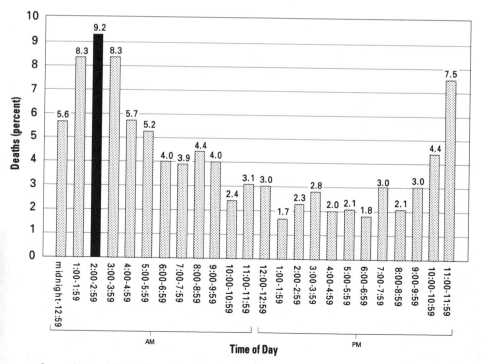

Source: National Fire Incidents Reporting System

Figure 3-6.

RESIDENTIAL FIRE INCIDENCE BY TIME OF DAY

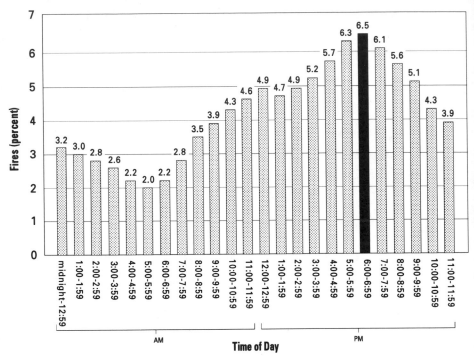

Source: National Fire Incidents Reporting System

Most deaths caused by fire happen late at night. Over half of the residential fire deaths occur between 11 P.M. and 6 A.M. Most people who die in fires die in their sleep. The worst hour is between 2 and 3 A.M.

Fire injuries, on the other hand, happen throughout the day. The most likely time for a fire injury is between 7 and 8 P.M. Unlike fire deaths, injury levels actually drop in the early morning hours when people are asleep. The peak hours of fire injury correspond to the hours when most people are preparing dinner. Fire incidence, which peaks from 6 to 7 P.M. also corresponds to meal times. Although fire dollar loss reaches its high point at the same time most fire deaths occur, like fire injuries, it drops in the early morning hours before dawn.

40

Winter, as might be expected, is the season when a home is most likely to catch fire and also the time when residential fire deaths are most likely to occur. In fact, a residential fire death is almost three times as likely to occur in January as in September. Nearly one-fourth of the entire year's fire deaths occur during the months of December and January alone. Heating is the main cause of the deaths, but other factors, such as holiday-related activities and increased alcohol consumption, also influence these statistics (Figure 3-7).

Figure 3-7.
RESIDENTIAL FIRE INCIDENCE BY MONTH

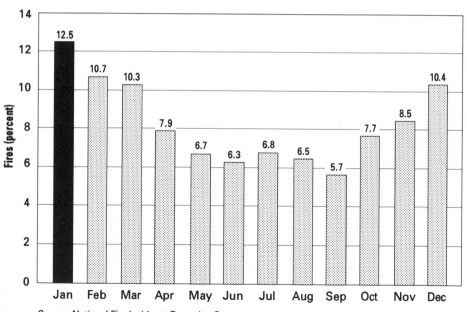

Source: National Fire Incidents Reporting System

WHERE FIRES OCCUR

Knowing where in the home fires typically occur can help in preventing injury, death, and financial loss (Figure 3-8). The most
likely area is the kitchen. Most fires are associated with cooking
over a stove or in the oven, but secondary areas, such as the exhaust
fan, can also be troublesome. The most common reason for fires in
the kitchen is that food has been left unattended during cooking.

Chimneys are the second most likely location for a home fire.
When chimneys are not cleaned on a regular basis, soot and creosote accumulate; this material itself can catch on fire.

Figure 3-8.

LEADING ROOMS OF ORIGIN FOR FIRES IN
ONE- AND TWO-FAMILY DWELLINGS

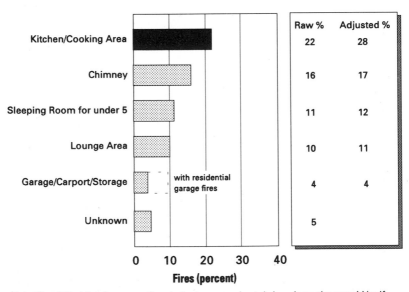

Note: The dotted line for garage fires indicates approximately how large they would be if
the residential garage portion of storage fires was added here. All of the other bars would
decrease and would have to be recomputed because the added garage fires would increase
the total number of fires by 6 percent.

Source: National Fire Incidents Reporting System

The third most likely location is the bedroom. In this living area, there are several leading factors, including—but not limited to— smoking in bed, children playing with matches, and arson. A typical scenario features a fire started by a child hiding under a bed or in a dark closet and igniting a match or cigarette lighter.

Garage and storage areas round out the list of the top five locations where fires start. Gasoline stored in unsealed containers leaks fumes that can travel along the floor and ignite upon contact with a spark or flame. About 20,000 such fires were reported in 1987 in the United States.

WHERE FIRE DEATHS OCCUR

For residential fire deaths, the breakdown is completely different. The most likely place for a person to die from a residential fire is in one of the lounging areas of the home, such as the living room. Typically, a careless smoker who has been drinking becomes intoxicated and falls asleep in a chair or couch holding a lighted cigarette that drops into the furniture and bursts into flames hours later. Contrary to what most people think, a person is more likely to be killed from careless smoking in the living room than the bedroom (Figure 3-9).

Bedrooms are the second most likely place for fire deaths. Again, smoking is a leading cause, but arson also plays a significant role, as does children playing with fire.

The kitchen is the third most dangerous room, and cooking is the leading cause.

 Forty thousand pets die in fires annually in the United States.

Figure 3-9.
LOCATION BY ROOM OF RESIDENTIAL FIRE DEATHS

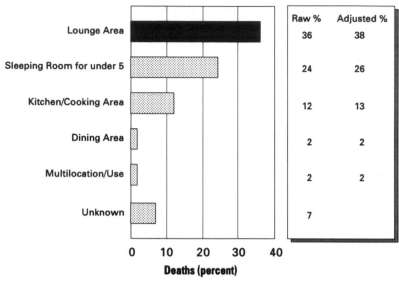

	Raw %	Adjusted %
Lounge Area	36	38
Sleeping Room for under 5	24	26
Kitchen/Cooking Area	12	13
Dining Area	2	2
Multilocation/Use	2	2
Unknown	7	

Source: National Fire Incidents Reporting System

Dining areas and multipurpose rooms complete the list; about two percent of all fire deaths occur there. For around seven percent of residential fire deaths, the place of the fire's origin is unknown.

Apartment Fires

Although the statistics cited above include residences of all types in the United States, they largely reflect one- and two-family dwellings, where three-quarters of the population lives. But many Americans—particularly those in urban areas—live in apartment buildings. These buildings, where numerous people from various backgrounds live under the same roof, have unique conditions that result in somewhat different causes for fires and fire deaths.

The most notable difference between one- and two-family homes and apartment buildings involves heating-related fires. Because most apartment buildings have centralized heating systems, heating ranks far lower as a cause of apartment fires than for fires in other types of residences.

As in dwellings of all types, careless smoking is the number one cause of fire deaths in apartments. However, the second and third leading causes of apartment fire deaths are different. After smoking, arson is the most common reason, followed closely by children playing with fire. Surprisingly, these three causes—smoking, arson, and children playing—account for over two-thirds of fire deaths in apartments. All other causes account for a relatively small percentage of all apartment fires. (See Figure 3-10.)

The causes of apartment fires are significantly different from causes for residences of all types. Heating, the single most likely source of fires in all residences, ranks number five as the cause of apartment fires. Cooking accounts for about one-third of all fires in

Figure 3-10.
CAUSES OF APARTMENT FIRE DEATHS

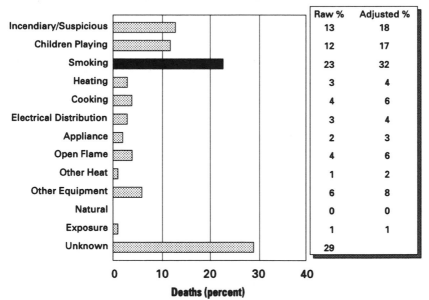

	Raw %	Adjusted %
Incendiary/Suspicious	13	18
Children Playing	12	17
Smoking	23	32
Heating	3	4
Cooking	4	6
Electrical Distribution	3	4
Appliance	2	3
Open Flame	4	6
Other Heat	1	2
Other Equipment	6	8
Natural	0	0
Exposure	1	1
Unknown	29	

Deaths (percent)

Source: National Fire Incidents Reporting System

apartments, followed by arson, smoking, and a category known as "other equipment," which includes maintenance equipment such as incinerators or elevators, computers, office machinery, and generators (Figure 3-11).

Apartment fire deaths follow the general profile for residences of all types: Fires that kill are most likely to occur in the early morning hours, while the most typical hour for a fire of any type to strike is during the dinner hours, due to the association with cooking.

One major difference is the lack of variance from month to month when fires occur. This reflects the fact that heating accounts for a smaller percentage of fires in apartments than in residences in general. Yet because many people stay home during the winter months (and smoke and drink) and because children may get bored

Figure 3-11.
CAUSES OF APARTMENT FIRES

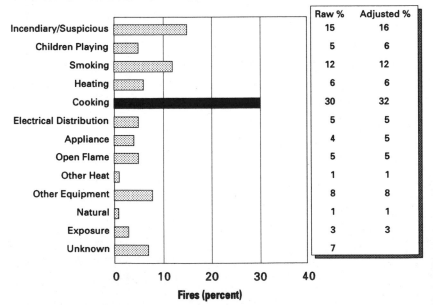

	Raw %	Adjusted %
Incendiary/Suspicious	15	16
Children Playing	5	6
Smoking	12	12
Heating	6	6
Cooking	30	32
Electrical Distribution	5	5
Appliance	4	5
Open Flame	5	5
Other Heat	1	1
Other Equipment	8	8
Natural	1	1
Exposure	3	3
Unknown	7	

Fires (percent)

Source: National Fire Incidents Reporting System

and start playing with matches for fun, winter is still the peak season for incidences of fire, although less dramatically so than in dwellings of all types.

Mobile Home Fires

Although the 10 million Americans who live in mobile homes represent only a small fraction of the population, they have a fire death rate that is double the national average. Over 500 people die every year in mobile home fires, and twice that many are seriously injured. Over 20,000 mobile home fires are reported annually. The dollar loss is in excess of $150 million.

To combat the problem, the U.S. Department of Housing and Urban Development established stringent fire safety standards for mobile homes in 1976. They have had a great impact. But while stricter national standards and major construction improvements by the industry (which prefers that the homes be called "manufactured housing") have dramatically reduced fire deaths, pre-1976 mobile homes still present unique fire hazards.

It's not hard to understand why older mobile homes are so vulnerable. Often, the exterior walls are made of aluminum siding. On the inside is a thin wall of paneling. Sandwiched in between is a slice of fiberglass insulation. When a fire breaks out in these homes, it can easily lead to disaster.

Like in most one- and two-family residences, heating problems are the number one cause of mobile home fires (Figure 3-12). For fire deaths, soking is the primary cause, just as it is in other residences (Figure 3-13).

One of the most critical safety issues involves the use of liquid petroleum (LP) gas. Many mobile homes—especially those in rural parts of the nation—use LP gas for heating, hot water, and cooking. LP gas is safe, but it has to be handled with extreme caution.

Containers of LP gas should never be stored inside the mobile

Figure 3-12.
CAUSES OF FIRES IN MOBILE HOMES

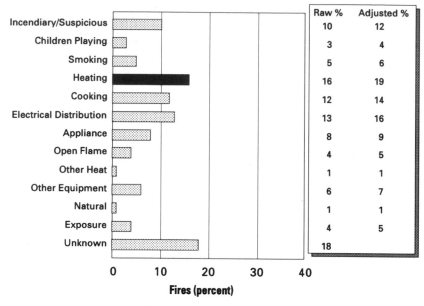

Source: National Fire Incidents Reporting System

home, not even for a very brief period of time. LP gas should always be kept outdoors at a distance of several feet away from the home and on a raised platform. If it is stored in a box on an outside wall of the mobile home, be sure that the box has sufficient ventilation. Keep leaves, dirt, and snow from blocking the vents on the box.

Each winter and summer, fuel lines should be checked for cracking due to the effects of extreme temperatures. If you live near heavy traffic or in an area that is prone to earthquakes, the lines should be checked for small cracks caused by tremors.

One difference between mobile homes and other one- and two-family houses is that electrical wiring represents the second leading cause of mobile home fires. Of course all homeowners need to be careful not to overload wiring, but mobile homes have an especially high percentage of fires related to electrical overloading.

Inside the mobile home, the usual rules of fire safety pertain. Extension cords should not run underneath carpets or across door-

Figure 3-13.
CAUSES OF FIRE DEATHS IN MOBILE HOMES

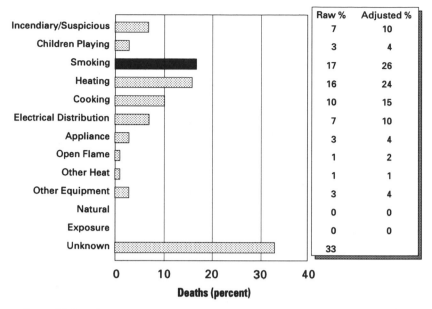

	Raw %	Adjusted %
Incendiary/Suspicious	7	10
Children Playing	3	4
Smoking	17	26
Heating	16	24
Cooking	10	15
Electrical Distribution	7	10
Appliance	3	4
Open Flame	1	2
Other Heat	1	1
Other Equipment	3	4
Natural	0	0
Exposure	0	0
Unknown	33	

Deaths (percent)

Source: National Fire Incidents Reporting System

ways, and they should never carry more load than they were designed for. This is particularly important for extension cords to power appliances that have a heating element, such as irons, toasters, refrigerators, hot plates, vaporizors, electric skillets, hair dryers, and popcorn poppers. If the wrong cord is used for these appliances, overheating can occur in less than an hour.

Every home should have smoke detectors. But because older mobile homes can be consumed so quickly in a fire, a well-maintained smoke detector is an absolute necessity.

Before installing a smoke detector in a mobile home, always try to locate it in the middle of the ceiling. If that's not possible, you need to decide which wall is best. The relatively thin exterior walls found in older mobile homes are not recommended. Try to choose a spot on an interior wall, away from heating and air-conditioning vents. If you have only one detector, place it near the bedrooms.

49

As with all homes, be sure that everyone in the family knows two escape routes from every room. Manufacturing requirements call for two exterior doors in every mobile home. Always keep these exits clear of obstacles.

Mobile homes have many advantages for homeowners, including modern designs that emphasize safety. And awareness of fire safety can help keep the mobile home experience a good one.

Hotel and Motel Fires

Because of new state and city laws and thanks to a broad industry effort, most American hotels and motels are protected by smoke detectors. In addition, most rooms have the added protection of sprinkler systems. Tragic disasters such as the New Year's Eve fire in the Dupont Plaza Hotel in San Juan and the MGM Grand Hotel fire in Las Vegas struck a note of alarm with the public. The industry has responded with strong programs to assure the safety of guests. The most significant result has been a continuing decline in the number of deaths and injuries in hotels and motels throughout the nation. In fact, rooming houses now account for more fire deaths annually than hotels and motels. Indeed, rooming houses together with hotels and motels account for far fewer annual incidents than residential fires.

At the same time, however, some unfortunate trends have emerged. Where once smoking was the number one cause of fires in hotels and motels, arson now ranks at about the same level as smoking. This is particularly disturbing because arson fires are so

 Men are almost twice as likely to die in a fire as women.

difficult to prevent. Arson accounts for twice as many fire deaths in hotels and motels as smoking. It should be noted, however, that unknown causes are so significant in hotel and motel fire deaths that, treated as a separate category, "unknown causes" ranks number one.

Most hotel and motel fires occur in individual guest rooms, usually as a result of careless smoking (often in conjunction with alcohol consumption) or arson caused by the guest or an employee.

Nonresidential Fires

Every year, about 200,000 fires are reported in nonresidential buildings. About one-third of them occur in offices and manufacturing plants, making those the most common locations for nonresidential fires. Although you might think that hospitals, jails, nightclubs, or nursing homes would account for more nonresidential building fires, it is only because fires in these places attract so much media attention that we expect them to rank higher in number of incidents.

The leading cause of fires in nonresidential buildings, as you might guess, is arson. In fact, arson accounts for nearly one-third of all fires and more than one-third of all dollar loss (see Table 3-1).

Automobile Fires

Although most of us are familiar with the well-publicized fires that have occurred in recent years in public places like hotels, few people are aware that outside of the home, the automobile is the most likely place for someone to be killed by fire. Vehicle fires account for 18 percent of all fire deaths, 13 percent of all fire

Table 3-1.
LEADING CAUSES OF NONRESIDENTIAL
FIRES AND DOLLAR LOSS

Property Type	Cause of Fire	Cause of Dollar Loss
Public Assembly	Arson	Arson
Eating, Drinking	Cooking (arson second)	Arson
Education	Arson	Arson
Institutions	Arson	Arson
Stores and Offices	Electrical (arson second)	Arson
Basic Industry	Other Equipment	Other Equipment
Manufacturing	Other Equipment	Other Equipment
Storage	Arson	Arson
Vacant/Construction	Arson	Arson
Outside and Unknown Structures	Arson	Arson

Source: National Fire Incidents Reporting System

injuries, 13 percent of dollar losses, and 24 percent of all reported fires.

Although the category of "vehicles" includes cars, trucks, vans, and tractor trailers, the vast majority of incidents occur in family automobiles—about seven out of eight. Additionally, fire deaths occur roughly three times more often in cars than in trucks. About 750 Americans are killed by fires in their cars every year.

The number one cause of vehicle fire deaths is collisions. In spite of the fact that collisions cause only two percent of all vehicle fires, 60 to 65 percent of all vehicle fire deaths result from collisions. By contrast, most fires in vehicles actually result from mechanical failure. Approximately one in six car fires is caused by arson, and this category is on the rise. "Carelessness" is given as the cause for only 13 percent of all vehicle fires, but it nonetheless is responsible for over one-fourth of the injuries. Typically, someone drops a cigarette in the car upholstery or mishandles gasoline during fillups or while working on the engine.

4

Children and Fire Safety

If you've ever gone through a burn ward and seen what fire can do to a child, it's a sight you will never forget.

—KENNETH KUNTZ
UNITED STATES FIRE ADMINISTRATION

In any situation, small children require special attention. But when it comes to fire safety, they represent an age group that demands extraordinary measures to ensure that they stay out of harm's way. In the hands of a toddler, a box of matches or a cigarette lighter becomes a lethal weapon (see Figure 4-1).

> In March 1991, Sophie B., a 29-year-old mother of two, died because her six-year-old daughter did not understand the power and danger of fire. The child had been playing with a cigarette lighter in her bedroom as her mother slept nearby with her other daughter, a two-year-old. Disposable cigarette lighters like these—with their wheels, sparks, colorful plastic containers, and dancing flames—make an inviting child's toy.
>
> Inevitably, a fire ignited amid the bedclothes. The girl tried to put it out herself, but the flames were overwhelming. She fled downstairs to her grandmother in the kitchen, pleading

Figure 4-1.

CAUSES OF FIRE DEATHS FOR CHILDREN UNDER 5 (ALL OCCUPANCIES)

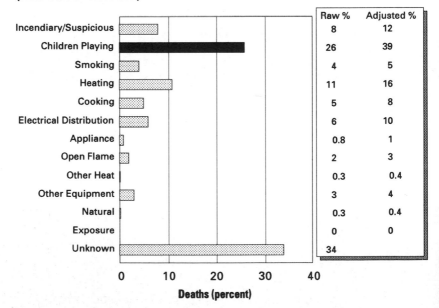

	Raw %	Adjusted %
Incendiary/Suspicious	8	12
Children Playing	26	39
Smoking	4	5
Heating	11	16
Cooking	5	8
Electrical Distribution	6	10
Appliance	0.8	1
Open Flame	2	3
Other Heat	0.3	0.4
Other Equipment	3	4
Natural	0.3	0.4
Exposure	0	0
Unknown	34	

Source: National Fire Incidents Reporting System

for her help. The grandmother screamed for the neighbors, but by then the room was engulfed in flames and Sophie and her two-year-old could not be saved. Besides dealing with the deaths, fire marshals at the scene had the burden of hearing the six-year-old, who survived the fire, tearfully confess what she had done.

Under similar circumstances, a three-year-old boy in Queens caused the death of his little sister by playing with a cigarette lighter. His mother was cooking dinner; his father was in the next room. The boy's grandmother was having an early supper in the dining room. The little boy ran downstairs, the grandmother later told fire officials, screaming "Fire! Fire!"

The parents tried to rescue their daughter, who was asleep upstairs, but the flames were too intense to enter the baby's room. Neighbors rigged up a ladder outside the building and smashed a window, but it was too late. Jessica—"a beautiful girl" is how her cousin described her—was pronounced dead at the hospital, a victim of second- and third-degree burns.

FIRE STATISTICS FOR CHILDREN
- Children often begin to play with fire around three years old.
- Children under age 10 represent 16 percent of the population but 23 percent of all fire deaths.
- Of all children killed in fires, one death out of four is due to playing with fire.
- Nearly half of all boys who die in fires are killed as a result of playing with fire.

The fire death rate for African-Americans is more than double the national average. The rate for Native Americans is even higher.

- Children playing with fire is the single largest cause of juvenile fire deaths.
- Approximately one in three child fire injuries is due to playing with fire.
- Eighty-five percent of the people who die in fires set by children are children.
- Two-thirds of all children who set fires are between the ages of five and nine.
- Children under age five have double the national average fire death rate.
- Every year 300 children are killed as a direct result of children playing with fire.
- The U.S. Consumer Product Safety Commission estimates that 140 people are killed annually from children playing with cigarette lighters.
- Children who play with fire cause almost $200 million in property damage every year.
- The second largest cause of children dying in fires is heating-related accidents. Arson is number three.

Why is fire so cruel to children? For one thing, very young children, like the elderly, have limited mobility. When a fire breaks out, they become trapped. It's significant that after age five, the death rate for children drops dramatically and is at its lowest between the ages of 10 and 14 (Figure 4-2). In large part, this is due to the fact that once they learn how to move, children are very fleet of foot.

The southeastern United States has the highest annual fire incidence rate in the country, with 9.9 fires per thousand population—about 16 percent higher than the national average.

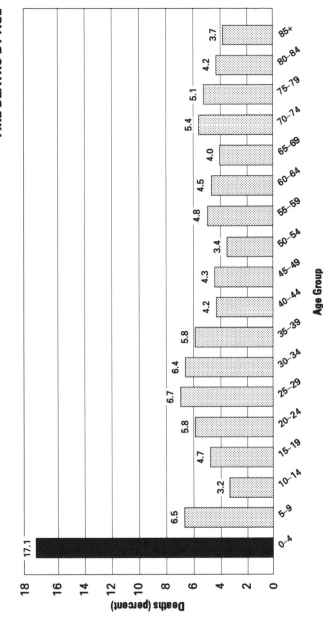

Figure 4-2.

FIRE DEATHS BY AGE

Source: National Fire Incidents Reporting System

For fire injuries, the trend is just the opposite. Even though young people are more able to escape a fire, their exposure increases dramatically with age, particularly for males. At age 20, a young adult is about one and a half times more likely to be injured in a fire than most other people. This increased risk is usually attributed to the fact that young adults—again, particularly males—make greater use of flammable liquids such as gasoline. The consumption of alcohol by males is also considered a factor (see Figure 4-3).

CURIOSITY KILLS

For small children, the greatest danger comes from curiosity. Children are naturally curious. They want to know how and why things work. And they begin to exercise that curiosity as soon as they have the ability to grasp and hold things in their hands.

Children first begin to show an interest in playing with matches around the age of three. Typically, a child gets hold of some matches or a cigarette lighter. He or she goes into a bedroom closet or crawls under the bed where the darkness creates the most exciting environment for fire play. After a few flickers of flame, a fire begins. The child panics and attempts to hide—only to die in the ensuing blaze.

The widespread use of disposable cigarette lighters makes playing with fire all the more accessible for children. Their bright-colored plastic casing makes them look like toys, and their flint wheels make traction devices that kids like to ''rev'' along tables, the floor, or their arms or legs.

What can you, as a parent or guardian, do to turn a child's natural curiosity away from the dangers of fire? Here are some tips from the Federal Emergency Management Agency, the U.S. Fire Administration, and the Insurance Information Institute for teaching young children about fire safety.

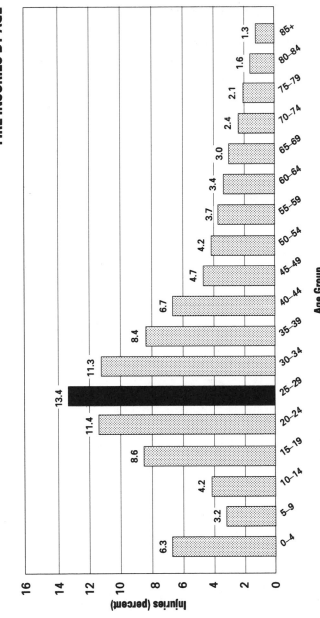

Figure 4-3.
FIRE INJURIES BY AGE

Age Group

Injuries (percent)

Age Group	Value
0–4	6.3
5–9	3.2
10–14	4.2
15–19	8.6
20–24	11.4
25–29	13.4
30–34	11.3
35–39	8.4
40–44	6.7
45–49	4.7
50–54	4.2
55–59	3.7
60–64	3.4
65–69	3.0
70–74	2.4
75–79	2.1
80–84	1.6
85+	1.3

Source: National Fire Incidents Reporting System

CHILD SAFETY CHECKLIST
- Keep matches and cigarette lighters out of reach.
- Remove lighters and matches from purses, which children like to explore.
- Instruct children always to tell you when they find matches or a cigarette lighter.
- Teach children to call for help immediately when they see a fire, no matter how small.
- Teach children never to hide when they see a fire.
- Tell children about the dangers of fire; don't assume they know.
- Teach by example. Show great care when handling fire. Never fool around with open flames.
- Never leave a lighted cigarette unattended.

HOW TO TALK TO YOUR CHILDREN ABOUT FIRE SAFETY

You don't have to be a firefighter to talk to children about fires. If you care for a child, you already know that even very young children can understand important subjects if they are handled properly. Small children should be taught fire safety in a serious yet entertaining way; most important, they should be taught in a way that won't scare them. Adult caregivers should address their preschoolers directly. Fire safety education is not a job for television and it's not a lesson that can wait until they're in school. Remem-

 Residents in rural communities with populations of less than 5,000 are more likely to be victims of fires than residents in cities with over a million population.

ber, fire is the number one cause of accidental death for children under age five in the United States.

The United States Fire Administration, in coordination with groups such as Safe Kids and the Children's Television Workshop, has developed recommendations for teaching children about fire safety. Their efforts have had an extremely positive impact on youngsters. By taking time to speak to your children personally, you can reinforce any fire safety messages they may receive from such outside sources, as well as offset any misleading information they may have picked up.

Here are some guidelines for teaching preschoolers about fire:

STOP, DROP, AND ROLL
- Tell your children about "stop, drop, and roll." Most preschoolers don't know what to do if their clothes catch fire. Teach them to place their arms by their sides; then, practice falling down and rolling until the fire is out. Demonstrate the procedure as you explain it.
- Three-year-olds usually need physical assistance in learning how to drop and roll before they can do it by themselves. Four-year-olds may need help too. Five-year-olds can usually understand without physical assistance.
- If the child has trouble grasping the concept, using a red paper "flame" may help. Be sure not to scare the child, though. If it looks as though the paper flame frightens the child, put it away.

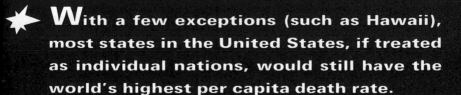

With a few exceptions (such as Hawaii), most states in the United States, if treated as individual nations, would still have the world's highest per capita death rate.

- Repeat the procedure until the child can stop, drop, and roll as an automatic response.

FIREFIGHTERS ARE FRIENDS

- Teach children that firefighters are their friends and that in case of a fire they shouldn't run away from them. To some children, firefighters in full gear resemble ''monsters.'' This is known as the ''Darth Vader syndrome.'' Showing them photographs of firefighters in full gear or taking them to visit a fire station can help preschoolers understand that despite their strange-looking outfits, firefighters are there to save them, not hurt them.

FIRE PREVENTION AND SURVIVAL

- Teach children that matches and cigarette lighters are dangerous. Instruct them never to touch these items and to come and tell you immediately if they find any.
- Teach your children an escape route. Show them at least one way to exit every room of the house at any time of the day or night. Practice your escape plan with them.
- Make sure your children can recognize the sound of the smoke detector.
- Teach your children how to roll out of bed—not sit or stand up—in case of a fire.
- Very young children may not be able to exit a building alone. Even so, teach them to stay low and crawl toward exits.
- Teach children to shout ''Fire!'' whenever they see a fire and call for help immediately. Tell them never to hide

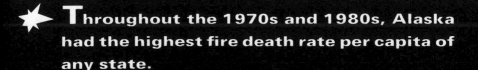

Throughout the 1970s and 1980s, Alaska had the highest fire death rate per capita of any state.

when they see a fire, but instead get away from it as fast as possible by leaving the house.

- Teach children to shout "Fire!" all during the time they are crawling toward an exit.
- Point out the word "Exit" to preschoolers. It's a simple word and appears often in public places. Teach them that this is the place to go in case of a fire.
- Consider placing Exit signs to indicate the escape routes out of your home. Glow-in-the-dark stickers placed low along the escape route might also help.
- Designate a safe place outside the home for everyone to gather in case of a fire. Tell children this is the place to go in a fire, nowhere else.

(For more information on fire safety for children, write: Children's Television Workshop, Department FS, 1 Lincoln Plaza, New York, NY 10023.)

THE YOUNG FIRE SETTER

The Federal Bureau of Investigation estimates that of every 10 people arrested for arson, four are juveniles. Some statistics have shown that about half of all fires set in the United States can be traced to juveniles. A New Jersey study indicated that as many as nine of 10 young fire setters are male.

The U.S. Fire Administration divides child fire setters into two main groups: the curiosity fire setter and the problem fire setter.

Curiosity Fire Setters

The curiosity fire setter is motivated by a desire to understand the world around him by experimentation. He is interested in finding out what a fire does, how it feels, how hot it is, and what it looks like. Typically, curiosity fire setters are male.

Here are some facts about curiosity fire setters:

> Children under the age of 10 are not likely to collect matches or cigarette lighters (termed ''fire tools'' by experts).
>
> Children who start fires usually wait around to watch the fire grow.
>
> Curiosity fire setters usually try to put out the fire themselves.
>
> A child under age 10 usually sets the fire close to home.
>
> Children over 10, because they are more mobile, are likely to set a fire away from home.
>
> Fires started by children over the age of 10 are rarely set to satisfy curiosity.
>
> One fire incident can be termed an ''accident''; multiple fire incidents are not accidents. If you see a repeat pattern, don't wait. Get help for your child.

Spanking a child for playing with matches is not the answer. Children need to be taught the dangers of fire and to be kept away from matches and cigarette lighters.

A three-year-old in Harlem died along with his two sisters in a fire started by playing with matches. ''We had been spanking him for playing with matches and lighters,'' a family

The first U.S. fire department was created by Peter Stuyvesant in New Amsterdam (later New York City) in 1648 when he distributed leather buckets, ladders, and hooks throughout the city.

friend told a reporter the next day. In a vain attempt to rescue the three children, one man tried to douse the fire with pails of water as flames leaped out of the room. He then threw down the pail and rushed into the room. He quickly emerged with burned arms, but he was unable to rescue the children.

Problem Fire Setters

The U.S. Fire Administration has developed two different profiles of problem fire setters—one for those between the ages of seven and 10 and one for those between the ages of 11 and 13. Their findings:

> Between the ages of seven and 10, problem fire setters collect fire tools.
> They usually set fires alone, but often work in pairs or groups.
> Fires are set close to home.
> Fire setting behavior is a reaction to problems at home or school.
> Fire setting may be used to get attention or to show anger.
> Most fire setters between the ages of seven and 10 admit to their actions and feel guilty.

Now, compare that profile with the one for older children:

> Between the ages of 11 and 13, problem fire setters collect fire tools.
> They act alone, in pairs, or in groups.
> Fire setting is a reaction to emotional stress.
> The parents may have alcohol and drug problems or trouble with the law.
> They often have very high or very low IQs.
> They are often malicious, disturbed, or angry.
> They sometimes set fires in response to peer pressure.

Juvenile fire setters constitute a significant part of the nation's growing arson problem. Juvenile and young adult fire setters account for nearly 60 percent of the fires in major urban areas. Two-thirds of all the fires begun in vacant buildings are started by teenagers aged 13 to 17. Most school fires are set by children between the ages of nine and 12.

A child is supposed to be curious, so a curiosity about fire should not be interpreted as a predisposition to become a fire setter. But even for those who play with fire just once, the chances of starting a larger fire are one in three. For children who repeatedly engage in fire play, the odds increase to an 80 percent chance of starting a serious fire.

If you think your child has a problem with fires—at any age— seek professional help as soon as possible. Talk to a school counselor, local fire department, or mental health professional. Many lives depend on it.

5

Surviving a Home Fire

When a fire breaks out in your home, you have precious little time to get yourself and your family out of danger. If you panic, you and your loved ones could die.

Figure 5-1 shows the leading causes of residential fire deaths and injuries. These are sobering statistics, but by learning now what to do in a fire, you can safeguard the health of your family. If you wait until a fire breaks out in your home, it's too late; the panic that can ensue will be your enemy. Besides damage to your property, you may suffer the ultimate loss—the death of yourself or a loved one.

Figure 5-1.

CAUSES OF RESIDENTIAL FIRE DEATHS AND INJURIES

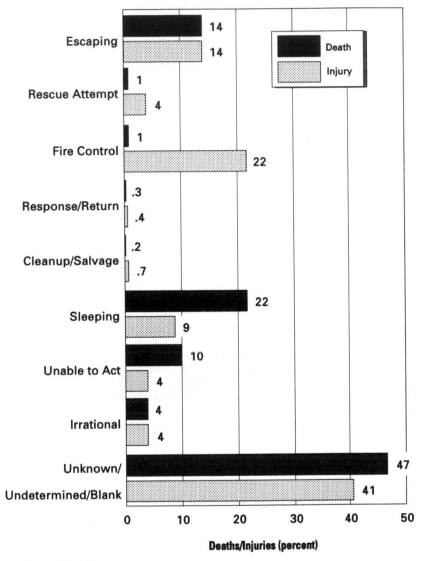

Source: National Fire Incidents Reporting System

By taking the time now to prepare for a fire, you will be miles ahead. No one can predict exactly when a fire will strike, but you can be ready if it does happen. In addition, you can greatly reduce the possibility of a fire by taking some simple, common-sense measures to protect your home.

WHEN THE SMOKE DETECTOR GOES OFF

One of the most likely scenarios is that the fire starts while you are asleep. Imagine that you're suddenly awakened from a deep sleep by the blare of your smoke detector. Knowing what to do in the first critical seconds after the alarm sounds can make the difference between life and death.

If you have a working smoke detector (see Chapter 6), you've already vastly increased your chances of survival. A smoke detector is your first line of defense. Remember: The majority of residential fire deaths occur in homes without working smoke detectors.

ONE- AND TWO-FAMILY HOUSE ESCAPE PLAN

1. When you first hear the alarm, roll off your bed and crawl onto the floor. Do not sit up in your bed. If there's smoke in the room, sitting up in bed or standing up may put you at a level where it is dangerous to breathe or expose you to tremendous heat that will instantly debilitate you. By staying low, you give yourself an opportunity to survive in a room that could otherwise be your death.

 New York City's fire department makes more fire runs per year than the entire nation of Japan.

2. Crawl to your bedroom door and feel it with the back of your hand. Do not collect any valuables or clothes. You and your family are the only valuables worth saving. If the door is hot to the touch, don't open it. It could mean that the fire is just outside of your door. Opening the door could bring a rush of flames into your room. Alternatively, opening the door could bring a gust of fresh oxygen to the flames and create a backdraft—the explosive fire that ignites everything and everybody in its path. A closed door makes a strong defense against fire and can give you protection until help arrives.

3. If the door is hot, seal the cracks around the door. Wet towels and blankets work best, but in an emergency, newspapers, clothes, or sheets will do.

4. Next, crawl to a window and open it slightly at the top and bottom. Opening a window all the way might pull smoke into your room from outside the door.

5. Break open a window only as a last resort. If you break a window and smoke is coming in from outside the home, there will be no way to close it. Also, a broken window may bring of rush of smoke from inside the home.

6. If you are on the first floor and can safely escape through the window, crawl out to safety. Above the first floor, don't consider jumping except as an absolute last resort. Many people who could have survived in a room while waiting for help to arrive have died by jumping from dangerous heights.

7. If you can't get out of your room, once you're at the window, make noise to let others know you are trapped inside. Banging objects together is better than shouting because it's important to save your breath. Waving a

U.S. firefighters have a death and injury rate that is among the highest in the world.

towel or sheet out the window will help signal your location.

8. If there is a phone in your room, call the fire department or 911 to report the fire and let them know that you are trapped inside.

9. Stay low by the window. This will allow you to breathe fresh air from the outside while avoiding the smoke that is likely to be seeping into your room from inside the house. Don't forget that poisonous carbon monoxide is colorless and odorless, so don't expect to see it or smell it.

10. If your bedroom door is not hot, open it slightly to look for smoke or flames.

11. After you leave your room, close the door. This will prevent the spread of the fire and help protect your property.

12. If the path looks clear, crawl along your predetermined escape route. Pound along the walls as you crawl and shout ''Fire!'' to alert others.

13. If possible, place a wet cloth over your nose and mouth before escaping. No matter what, stay low.

14. Don't look for the fire. The precious time you spend searching for a fire may be the same moments you need to escape the home.

15. Unless you are trapped in a room with a phone, don't take time to call the fire department before escaping. Many people have died while calling the fire department. Remember, you don't have time in a fire.

 About 40 percent of all firefighter deaths are caused by heart attacks. Two-thirds of those deaths occur in firefighters over 45 years old.

16. Go directly to your family's predetermined meeting place outside of the home. Don't wait for everyone to meet in the house before escaping. Once you are outside, call the fire department (never assume that it has been done by a neighbor). Stay on the line until the department has all the information they need. If you are at an alarm box, stay by the box in case you need to direct the fire truck to the fire.
17. Don't go back into the house until the fire department determines it's safe to return.

APARTMENT AND HIGH-RISE ESCAPE PLAN

1. If the fire is not in your apartment, call the fire department—but only if you are not in immediate danger.
2. If your floor is on fire, exit the building, closing all doors behind you. If you are not on the fire floor or the floor directly above, stay put until you receive other instructions from fire personnel.
3. If you must exit, take your keys. If you cannot escape the building because you are trapped by smoke or flames, you'll need the key to return to your apartment, which may be your safest refuge.
4. Sound your building's fire alarm.
5. Don't stand in the hallways wondering what to do, even if you perceive no immediate danger. Get out.
6. Know which apartment corridors are dead ends and stay away from them.
7. Always use the stairs, never use the elevator. Elevators are sometimes designed to respond to heat and will

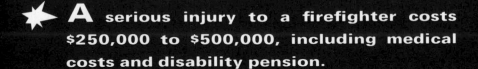

A serious injury to a firefighter costs $250,000 to $500,000, including medical costs and disability pension.

automatically go to the fire floor. Also, the elevator can
act as an air shaft, becoming a chimney for a fire. Walk
downward. Go to the roof only as a last resort.

8. Expect others to panic, so hold on to the handrail of the
   stair as you exit. It will keep you from being knocked
   over if there is a stampede in the stairwell.

9. If you are trapped in your apartment, stay inside and
   follow the procedures outlined above.

10. Don't jump.

11. Walk, don't run. Running causes others to panic.

(See also Chapter 11.)

REACTING TO FIRE

If you are in a room where a fire starts, you may be able to extinguish it yourself. But don't try unless you know what you're doing.
Improper handling of a fire may put you and others at a greater risk
than if you do nothing.

GENERAL GUIDELINES

1. If you see a small fire burning in a room, realize that
   you may have only 30 seconds in which to extinguish
   the blaze.

2. If a fire extinguisher is within a few steps, use it to
   extinguish a small blaze. It is extremely important to
   know how to use the extinguisher. Improper use of the
   extinguisher can actually make the situation worse and
   spread the flames. If you're not sure, don't use the
   extinguisher, just escape.

3. In the kitchen—the most likely place for a fire in the
   home—use a pot lid to extinguish a grease fire. Never
   use flour, because it could explode. Alternatively,
   smother the flames with a large amount of baking soda.
   Be prepared for a flareup after it appears the flames are

out. You can also use a fire extinguisher designed for grease fires.

4. Besides the oven and stove, the electric exhaust fan is a prime area for fires to start. Use only a grease and electrical fire extinguisher (type BC) or all purpose (type ABC) to put out such fires (see Chapter 11).

5. If you cannot control a fire within 30 seconds, get out. Any additional time you take to fight the blaze is likely to be in vain and could put you and others in unnecessary danger.

6. If you have gas appliances, such as a stove, water heater, or furnace, beware of gas leaks. If you smell a faint odor (natural gas is odorless, but sulfur—to which the nose is extremely sensitive—is added as a safety precaution) open the windows and doors to ventilate the area. If you detect the smell next to a natural gas appliance, turn off the gas valve.

7. If the smell of gas is strong, never search for the source. Instead, open the windows and leave immediately. If you use the telephone to call the fire department, ring a doorbell, flip a light switch, or even click on a flashlight, the gas may be ignited by electrical sparks. Alert everyone in the area to evacuate. The explosive power of natural gas is similar to a bomb. Once you have evacuated the area, call the fire department.

8. If your clothes catch on fire, don't panic or flail your arms. This will only spread the flames. When clothes catch on fire, stop, drop to the ground, and roll back and forth. If a blanket or rug is within close reach, grab it

 The average U.S. fire department spends under three percent of its budget on fire prevention.

and wrap it around you. Don't waste time looking for a blanket or rug. It can mean the difference between survival and severe injury.

9. If you see someone on fire, don't assume that he or she is aware of it or knows enough about fire to stop, drop, and roll. Instead, tell the person that she is on fire, then pull her to the ground, and roll her back and forth until the flames are out. Act quickly. It only takes 10 seconds for fire to spread from the hemline to the neckline. If a blanket or rug is handy, it can be used to smother the flames. Or use your jacket.

10. If you must jump into a fire safety net, jump in a sitting position.

6

Home Fire Prevention

If a fire occurs in your home you will have only a precious few seconds to escape. There won't be time to determine an escape plan. There won't be time to decide alternate routes. It will be too late to install a smoke detector or to learn how to use a fire extinguisher. Now is the time to become familiar with the tools of fire prevention and to learn the essentials of fire safety.

SMOKE DETECTORS

The introduction of smoke detectors into the American home has revolutionized the fight for fire safety. By emitting harmless rays that scan for smoke, detectors provide an early warning that gives you time to escape a fire before it's too late. Today 80 percent of all fire deaths occur in homes without functioning smoke detectors or without any detectors at all.

Some experts estimate that from one-tenth to one-third of all smoke detectors do not function properly because the batteries are dead or have been removed. Sometimes a smoke detector goes off too often—usually in response to cooking smoke—and the annoyance leads people to remove the battery. This is a dangerous trade-off. If your smoke detector is tripped too frequently by cooking smoke, consider moving it farther away from the cooking source—but not so far that a fire in the kitchen can't be detected. Remember, the kitchen is one of the most likely areas for a fire in the home.

It is extremely important to know how many smoke detectors your home needs and where to put them. Also, buy smoke detectors that are UL approved. (See Chapter 11 for further information on installation and types of detectors available.)

PLACEMENT OF SMOKE DETECTORS

Deciding where to place smoke detectors depends on the physical layout of your home and your family's lifestyle (Figures 6-1 and 6-2). Use the following checklist to help you figure out where to put your smoke detectors:

- How many floors are in your home? A good rule of thumb is that you need at least one smoke detector for every floor, possibly more.

Figure 6-1.

SMOKE DETECTOR PLACEMENT IN A SINGLE-STORY HOME

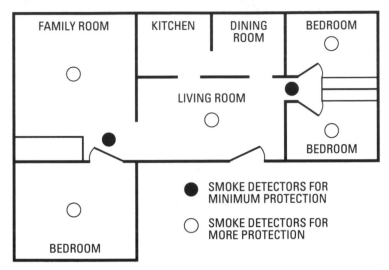

Source: First Alert

Figure 6-2.

SMOKE DETECTOR PLACEMENT IN A TWO-STORY HOME

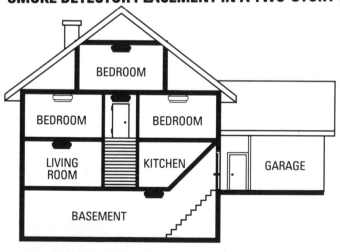

Source: First Alert

- Does any member of your family smoke in the bedroom? Smokers should have detectors in their bedrooms.
- Do any household members sleep with the bedroom door closed? Each room that has its door closed at night should also have its own smoke detector.
- Do you or a family member use the garage or other area as a work room? Work areas are particularly susceptible to fire and need smoke detectors.
- If your hallways are longer than 40 feet, place a smoke detector at each end.
- Know what the smoke detector alarm sounds like. If you have children, let them watch you test it so that they also recognize the sound of the alarm. In this day of car alarms, ambulance sirens, and microwave oven beeps, don't assume that anyone will recognize the smoke detector alert—hear it for yourself and be sure.
- Test your smoke alarm regularly. Most units are powered by a battery or by AC power. If your detector is powered by a battery, test each unit every six months. Pick a consistent date—your birthday and another annual event will do. Another alternative is to check detectors in the spring and fall when the clocks change to and from Daylight Savings Time. It only takes a few minutes, and it could save your life.
- Smoke detectors manufactured since 1980 have a test button you can push to check the alarm. The button tests not only the battery but the entire unit.
- If your smoke detectors are AC-powered, check them every month, perhaps on the day you change the calendars.

 The average fire department in Western Europe allocates between 4 and 10 percent of its budget to fire prevention.

ESCAPE PLANS AND FIRE DRILLS

No matter how careful you are, or how safe you've made your home, the best way to prevent injury and death is to make an escape plan in case of fire. Begin by reviewing the escape plans in Chapter 5 with your family.

Ideally, you should practice your escape plan under the circumstances that are likely to occur in the event of a fire. The best way to begin is to draw a floor plan of your home, including every floor and room in the home. Include every door and window in every room. Make it a family project. When a fire strikes, it's too late to encourage participation. Have each member of the family identify at least two exits from each room, especially bedrooms.

It's particularly important that children be protected from fires. Fires kill and injure more children annually than any disease. You wouldn't think of letting your child go without necessary vaccines. Don't leave them susceptible to fire.

Next, practice fire drills in the home—and practice them in the way you would act in case of a fire. An effective fire drill is the best way to test you and your family.

Try this experiment: With the help of a partner, go to your bedroom and close your eyes. Then, turn around several times until you're not sure in which direction you're pointing. With your eyes still closed, drop to your hands and knees. Now try to exit the room using the two escape routes you've mapped out in case of a fire. In a real fire, you can expect to be disoriented, blinded by smoke, and crawling to escape the heat and smoke overhead. If you find it hard

 Over two million fires are reported annually in the United States.

to escape during practice with the help of a partner, imagine what it would be like in a real emergency.

An effective fire drill involves actually going through the same routine you will follow in an emergency. The following checklist outlines some of the steps you and your family can take in preparation for the unexpected.

FIRE DRILL CHECKLIST

1. Have each member of the family practice rolling out of bed (as opposed to sitting up in bed or standing up) and crawling to both escape routes. Practice feeling the door to determine if it is hot.
2. Remind family members that in the event of a fire they must not try to save their clothes, valuable papers, jewelry, or any other precious items. Their job is to alert other members of the family and get out as fast as possible.
3. Keep a working flashlight beside each person's bed. Because fire is pitch black, a flashlight can make a critical difference.
4. Stress the importance of closing doors behind them as family members leave the home. Closed doors make it more difficult for the fire to spread and could save lives and property damage.
5. Remind everyone that the time to call the fire department is not before they've escaped the home, but after they're outside. Many people have died while trying to call the fire department from inside a burning building.
6. Establish a central meeting place outside the home where everyone will gather in the event of a fire. This critical step in the plan will keep family members from worrying unnecessarily about who else might be trapped inside. Too often, people race back into a home to save family members who are already safe—only to die in the

unnecessary rescue. Although everyone should take
responsibility to alert others to the fire, the most
important thing is for each individual to get outside
alone.

7. Remind everyone that it is vital to stay outside the
   home and not return for any reason.
8. If there are family members who would not be able to
   get out by themselves—such as small children, the
   elderly, or the severely physically impaired—determine
   how they will escape and who will assist them and
   practice this procedure.
9. If you keep fire extinguishers in the home (and you
   should) be sure that everyone who is able to operate
   them knows how (see Chapter 11). A fire extinguisher
   can be dangerous if not handled properly.
10. Check to see if it's safe to escape via the windows.
    Even first-floor windows sometimes present hazards. To
    test their viability as escape routes, try climbing in the
    windows from the outside.
11. Alert everyone to the dangers of jumping out of high
    windows.
12. Practice stuffing cloth or newspapers around doorjambs
    to keep out smoke in case someone is trapped in a
    room.
13. Check each window to see if it will open.

REMOVING HAZARDS FROM THE HOME

Fires in the home are not an act of God. They are the result of
human carelessness. Most of them could have been prevented.

 Approximately 20 million fires go un-
reported every year in the United States.

Use the following checklist to determine whether your home is fire safe.

HOME SAFETY CHECKLIST
1. Keep matches and cigarette lighters away from children and out of their reach. Remember, three-year-old children are the most likely of any age group to be killed from playing with matches.
2. Make sure all replacement fuses are the right size for your fuse box. Improper fuses can bring excess power into the wiring, causing overheating—a fire hazard.
3. Check all electrical cords to see if any are hung over a nail or placed under carpeting or furniture. Replace all frayed and cracked cords.
4. Check to see if any electrical cords or outlets are overloaded with too many appliances.
5. Make sure that thin extension cords are not being used to carry power to large appliances, such as an air conditioner or a refrigerator.
6. Install a smoke detector in the bedroom of each person who smokes.
7. Make a rule against smoking in bed.
8. Always use large metal or ceramic ashtrays.
9. Keep the kitchen stove, oven, and exhaust fan free of grease buildup.
10. Make sure curtains never hang too close to a heat source, such as the stove, oven, fireplace, space heater, or hot water heater.
11. Keep a large pot lid and a supply of baking soda handy in the kitchen for extinguishing grease fires.
12. Never use charcoal to cook inside the home or in any enclosed area, such as the carport or garage.
13. Remind each family member—particularly the young and old—of the hazards of wearing loose-fitting clothing near flames.

14. If you use a wood-burning stove or fireplace, clean the chimney regularly.
15. Make sure the connecting pipe coming out of the wood-burning stove is the same size as the connecting pipe going into the chimney.
16. Never use a gas oven to heat the house. It can rob the room of oxygen and lead to a buildup of carbon monoxide.
17. Be sure the design of any heating device includes a mechanism that will automatically turn it off if it overheats or is overturned and that the device is otherwise safe.
18. Use extreme caution with kerosene heaters (or any portable heater) in the home. Besides being a potential fire hazard, they can lead to carbon monoxide buildup and decrease oxygen, resulting in asphyxiation.
19. Never place heaters close to anything flammable, including blankets, curtains, or rugs.
20. Be sure all space heaters carry the Underwriters Laboratories (UL) label or other nationally recognized testing laboratory label.
21. Always store flammable liquids in tightly closed containers. Keep them away from heat sources. Fumes can travel far from their containers.
22. Remove any potentially flammable debris from your home—e.g., piles of raked leaves around the foundation, oily rags in the garage, stacks of old newspapers in the attic. Wet newspapers are flammable, too. As they decompose, they generate heat that can cause them to combust.
23. Use electric blankets carefully. Don't place anything on one or fold it over on top of itself during use.

 Residential fires account for about 80 percent of all fire deaths.

HOLIDAY SAFETY

The holidays are a time of great joy, but many of them are also associated with fire hazards—candles on birthdays, Chanukah, Christmas, and Kwanza; electric lights at Christmas; bonfires and barbecues on the Fourth of July; jack-o'-lanterns and costumes at Halloween. In addition, fireworks are becoming a part of more and more celebrations.

Another critical feature of the holidays is alcohol use. Alcohol is associated with many fire deaths, because it interferes with the exercise of common sense. When smoking is added, the combination can prove deadly.

During the holidays, think before you create an event and ask yourself if you might be creating a fire hazard instead. Use the holiday checklists below to determine if all your planned activities are safe.

CHRISTMAS CHECKLIST
- Pick a Christmas tree that is fresh. A fresh tree has flexible branches and needles that resist shedding when stroked.
- Before you place your tree in a water container, saw off the bottom two inches of the trunk to allow water to feed the tree. Replenish the water often.
- Never put lighted candles on a tree.
- Avoid old-fashioned large lightbulbs, which tend to dry out the tree's branches and needles. Use miniature lights instead.
- Never put electric lights on a metal tree.
- Whenever the family leaves the home or goes to bed at night, unplug the tree lights.
- Don't burn your tree at the end of holiday. Mulch it instead.
- Never smoke near the tree.
- Don't let giftwrap pile up beneath the tree near the lights.

- Avoid placing the tree too close to a heat source such as a radiator or space heater.

CHANUKAH CHECKLIST
- Any item that involves candles, such as a menorah, should be treated as an open fire.
- Never place any flammable object near a lighted menorah.
- Never leave a lighted menorah unattended.
- Be sure that children understand the fire hazard created by the candles.

FOURTH OF JULY CHECKLIST

Fireworks are the most dangerous part of Independence Day celebrations. Every year, hundreds of adults and children are injured and some are killed. Fireworks that misfire can destroy property and endanger everyone in the vicinity. Many communities and states have laws restricting or prohibiting fireworks. Be sure that every member of your family obeys these laws, and share these guidelines with them.

- Go only to legal fireworks displays.
- Hold small children by the hand while watching the display.
- Don't get too near the display.
- If you see illegal fireworks being used, stay away.
- Never hold fireworks in your hand.
- Remember that even though sparklers have a reputation of being safe, they can burn and can start fires.

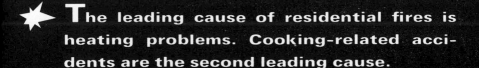

The leading cause of residential fires is heating problems. Cooking-related accidents are the second leading cause.

HALLOWEEN CHECKLIST

Halloween is meant to be scary, but it should never be life-threatening. Whenever an open flame is used, the situation has the potential for danger.

- Make sure all costumes are flame-retardant. Be sure costumed children can see clearly and move easily and safely.
- Never allow children to carry a candle or any other open flame.
- Never leave a jack-o'-lantern unattended. The hot wax inside the pumpkin is a fuel source that can cause a table or any other flammable material to catch fire.

7

Fire Safety for the Disabled

The disabled form one of the largest groups in the United States at risk of dying in a fire. They are particularly vulnerable to fires because they are less able to escape. We can reduce these risks by using quick response sprinklers and more sensitive smoke detectors. We must also build homes designed to make entrances and exits accessible for individuals using wheelchairs or walkers. Providing better fire safety and protection must be of utmost concern to all Americans.

—ALEXANDER PIRNIE
PRESIDENT, NEW YORK BOARD OF FIRE UNDERWRITERS

Fire safety is everyone's concern, but for those with physical or mental challenges, it requires extra care and preparation.

According to the 1992 Americans with Disabilities Act, over 43 million Americans have some sort of disability—a condition that seriously limits their mobility or the use of their senses or mental functions. Two million disabled people are cared for in institutions, but the vast majority of people with disabilities live under the same residential conditions as the able-bodied. About one and a half million Americans use wheelchairs. About two million have significant visual impairment. Many others suffer from hearing loss, and still others have limited use of one or more limbs. About eight million Americans have a mental disability.

Fortunately, several organizations, including local fire departments such as Nassau County, New York, have developed fire safety programs for the disabled. One such organization is the Eastern Paralyzed Veterans Association, based in Jackson Heights, New York City.

One of their members, a quadriplegic with severely limited use of his body, was caught in a fire. The man, who used an electric wheelchair equipped with special controls, was largely dependent on the assistance of an aide. One holiday season, malfunctioning Christmas decorations ignited a fire in his home. His smoke detector had been dismantled. To make matters worse, no one had ever mapped out an escape plan. When the fire broke out, his aide discovered that the residence lacked sufficient exits. Panic set in, and the veteran perished in the fire.

After this unfortunate accident, the Eastern Paralyzed Veterans Association decided to tackle the issue with a brochure that focused on the special needs of all those with limited physical mobility. They are to be commended for taking the lead in this area. (Anyone wishing to obtain a free copy of their brochure, "Wheeling to Fire Safety," can call EPVA at 1-800-444-0120.)

In listening to discussions about fire safety for the handicapped, I'm often astonished to hear comments such as "They account for such a small percentage of the population, it's hard to do anything for them" or "You can't save everybody." But organizations such as this veterans' group show that you can do something for the handicapped by focusing not on their disabilities, but instead on their abilities.

HAVE AN ESCAPE PLAN

Oddsmakers estimate that all of us—disabled or not—will face up to three major fires in our lives. The best way to prepare for a fire emergency is to start before the fire strikes. Knowing what to do will preclude panic and give the disabled person the confidence to handle any emergency that arises.

The most important factor in making the disabled fire safe is to be sure there is a working smoke detector in the home. Detectors are especially important for those with disabilities, because they often need extra time to get out. As always, the smoke detector is the first line of defense and fire extinguishers can be lifesavers.

If possible, assign someone who lives with the disabled person to help him or her get out in case of an emergency. Aides should practice fire drills with the disabled person and know what to do in case critical equipment—such as wheelchairs or electrical equip-

 A cigarette can smolder in furniture for three or four hours before bursting into flames.

ment—should fail. Planning in advance for an alternative will avert disaster.

Even if there is an aide, the disabled person must be shown how to be responsible for his or her own safety. Putting someone else in charge of a person's rescue won't do any good if the rescuer is incapacitated by flames or smoke. Besides, having the confidence of knowing what to do in case of a fire, whether a helper shows up or not, can prevent panic and keep the disabled person alive.

If a person is immobile, the room should have sprinklers to best assure the person's safety. In case of a fire, you should use the stairs, since an elevator could expose you to smoke or bring you to the floor with the fire. But people in wheelchairs must be provided with alternatives to stairs. If a disabled person has sufficient upper body strength, he or she should be prepared to crawl down the stairs. In addition, a mechanic's crawler should be kept under the bed to allow those with limited upper body strength to pull themselves from disaster.

For disabled people, it is especially important to minimize obstacles. For instance, those with physical limitations can eliminate the need to negotiate stairs by living and sleeping on the ground floor. If the bedroom is located on the side of the residence where firefighters are likely to be stationed, the disabled person will have greater access to help.

Windows, as the secondary exit for the disabled, should be easy to open. Oversized windowsills, jammed windows, and other obstacles should be eliminated. If the distance from the window to the ground is dangerously high, a ramp or ledge can be built.

Another way to prepare ahead of time is to notify the local fire department that someone in your home has a physical limitation. Ask them for recommendations on making the home safe, and let them make note of where disabled persons sleep.

The bedroom of a disabled person should always have a telephone beside the bed. A whistle should also be kept by bedside. The whistle can be used to call for help in case the person is trapped inside.

If the person uses a cane, an extra cane should be kept next to fire exits. Be sure that all doors that might be used for escape swing outward.

In the event that a person with physical limitations is trapped inside a room, he or she must know how to keep smoke out of the room and how to signal for help. It may be necessary to soak a cloth with water and breathe through it. He or she should be aware that a closed door is the single best defense in keeping fire at bay. It is also important to keep a white cloth handy for signaling neighbors. A portable supply of oxygen can also keep someone alive until help arrives. But don't forget that oxygen is extremely flammable, so use it with care and never while smoking.

For those with hearing impairment, a smoke detector attached to strobe sensors is the best way to alert sleepers.

DISABLED BUT ABLE

When it comes to moving bedridden or wheelchair-bound people, it's not always necessary to carry them in your arms. You can shift them onto a blanket and drag them to safety. Alternatively, place the person into a chair, then tilt the chair and drag it out. If two people are making the carry, the chair makes it easier to transport the person.

If the person is smaller than you, you can, of course, scoop him

 Careless smoking is the fifth leading cause of residential fires, but it is the number one cause of residential fire deaths.

or her up in your arms. But even if the person is your size or slightly larger, you can carry him or her by the following method: Turn the person on her side. Back up against her midsection. Place her left arm over your shoulder and pull it down. With your right arm behind her back and your left arm behind her legs, pull her around your body at your waistline (not below, because she will slip off). Bend slightly forward, knees apart, and heft the person onto your back. This will permit you to carry the person with a minimum of difficulty.

For those who are visually impaired, the bedroom is usually set up in such a way that they know how to get around simply by the sense of touch. Ironically, those with limited vision are not handicapped by the blackness of a fire, because they are accustomed to not seeing. However, if trapped in a room by fire, everyone—including the visually impaired—should turn on the light to let those outside know that someone is inside.

8

Fire Safety for the Elderly

Like so many other misfortunes, fire attacks the old and young with disproportionate fury. The reasons are simple. These two age groups often represent those whose mobility is most limited.

Older people, however, present a different kind of fire risk than youngsters. There are over 25 million Americans 65 and older. And while babies and small children are in the care of others, many elderly people live alone or with just one other person, often another older person.

Of the nearly 6,000 Americans killed annually in fires, about one-fourth are over the age of 60. Tens of thousands of people over the age of 65 are injured in fires every year. The odds of becoming a fire casualty are twice as high for the elderly as for the population in general.

Because the skin of older people is thin, they are more susceptible to burns. Their decreased sensitivity sometimes allows burns to injure the skin before action is taken to stop the burning.

As with all age groups, it's not only the burns that are the problem but also the smoke and toxic fumes. Here, too, older people are particularly vulnerable. Weakened respiratory systems magnify the already deadly dangers of smoke.

Smoke can lull anyone into a deeper sleep, but it is particularly lethal to older Americans. Statistics show that almost half of the elderly killed in fires were asleep at the time of fire. Therefore, a smoke detector is crucial for the fire safety of older Americans; a recent study revealed that 80 percent of all elderly people who died in fires did not have a working smoke detector.

HAVE AN ESCAPE PLAN

However, a smoke detector is simply an early warning device. It can't extinguish flames, and it won't transport a person out of a burning building. That is why older people, like everyone else, must be prepared for a fire before it happens. This is essential for their safety, especially if they live alone, since they will have to know how to save themselves.

Elderly people who live alone should always alert their local fire department to this fact and ask them to make note of whether or not they would need special assistance to escape a fire emergency. The fire department should also note where the person sleeps.

It is important for an older person to practice two ways to escape from every room. Sometimes he or she will need to escape via an open window. Older people need to have the confidence to be able to climb out a window *before* a fire strikes. An emergency is no time to test your ability. But even in practice, never take an unnecessary risk that can cause injury.

An elderly person, like others, may become trapped in the bedroom if the doorway is blocked by fire. To prepare for this consequence, he or she should know how to open the window slightly, how to use wet cloths pressed over the nose and mouth to keep from breathing smoke, how to block smoke from seeping in around the door, and how to signal to people outside the house.

An older person may feel that it's undignified to go through a fire drill, but even one practice drill will provide a great advantage in escaping a fire. The smoke often makes fire victims feel disoriented and confused. When a fire strikes, there is no time to figure out an escape plan.

Keep essential items next to the bed at all times. Included should be a whistle—which lets rescuers know where you are and also alerts your housemates that there is trouble—glasses (if needed), a

 Contrary to popular belief, fires caused by careless smoking do not occur only in the bedroom. They can occur in any room in the house.

flashlight, and a telephone. Phone numbers for the fire and police departments should be written in large letters so that they can be read without glasses and kept next to the phone. Even better, memorize the fire department's phone number in addition to writing it down.

It's a good idea to sleep with the door closed, too. In case of fire outside the bedroom, a closed door can keep the fire at bay for an hour or even longer.

Avoid using space heaters in the bedroom. If you do use them, keep at least three feet of space clear all around them. Never use a space heater to dry clothing, and always turn off the heater before you go to sleep. Because of their association with so many fire tragedies, avoid using kerosene heaters. If you use any appliance that burns fuel (whether it's wood, coal, propane, or kerosene), be sure it has proper ventilation to the outdoors. The fumes from these devices can be deadly, and improperly vented heaters can suffocate you.

If you use electric blankets, be sure they are in good condition, without cracks or breaks in the wiring, cord, or plug. Check for charred spots on both sides of the blanket. Never place anything on top of a blanket that's in use—not another blanket, not a sleeping pet, nothing. This can cause the blanket to overheat. Don't fold the blanket over on top of itself during use; this, too, can cause overheating.

KITCHEN SAFETY

The emotional and psychological effects of aging are as important as the physical changes. Not only do some older people move more slowly, they sometimes think more slowly or find it hard to concentrate. Sometimes they are forgetful. This can lead to dangers throughout the home, but particularly in kitchens. As Figure 8-1 shows, cooking-related accidents are the number one cause of fire injuries in people over 70.

Not everyone lives in a house, but regardless of the type of home—apartment, condominium, mobile home, or senior residence—most elderly people have kitchens. Thanks to the same appliances that make cooking so convenient, the kitchen can be the most dangerous room in the house. The use—and misuse—of appliances contributes to a staggering percentage—about 20 percent—of home fires. All too often, the victim is an elderly person.

One way to ensure that food isn't left to burn on the stove or in

Figure 8-1.

CAUSES OF FIRE INJURIES FOR ELDERLY OVER 70 (ALL OCCUPANCIES)

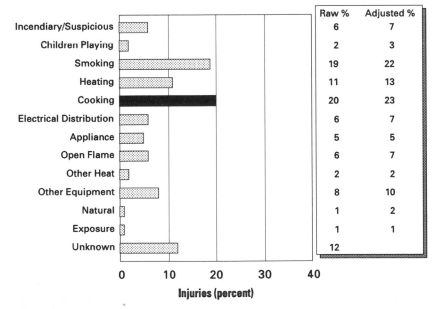

	Raw %	Adjusted %
Incendiary/Suspicious	6	7
Children Playing	2	3
Smoking	19	22
Heating	11	13
Cooking	20	23
Electrical Distribution	6	7
Appliance	5	5
Open Flame	6	7
Other Heat	2	2
Other Equipment	8	10
Natural	1	2
Exposure	1	1
Unknown	12	

Injuries (percent)

Source: National Fire Incidents Reporting System

the oven due to forgetfulness is to stay in the kitchen while it is cooking. If that's not convenient, set a bell timer whenever you leave the kitchen as a reminder to return. Another method is to carry a potholder or wooden spoon to remind you that you're cooking.

One of the most tragic scenerios for older people in the kitchen is when their clothes catch on fire. Although everyone should be aware of the dangers of wearing loose clothing around fire sources, elderly people need to be especially careful.

> While preparing her morning coffee, one California grandmother caught the sleeve of her nightgown on fire when she reached over a lighted burner. The woman panicked. She ran to the front door and screamed for help. Instead of dropping to the ground and rolling until the flames were out, she then ran to the back door of the house, still screaming. By the time help arrived, the woman was wrapped in flames that had been fanned by her movements. She died soon afterward.

"Stop, drop, and roll" is not for kids only.

Tightly woven natural fabrics that are not loose on the body offer the best protection against catching on fire. Synthetics burn easily; often, they melt and stick to the skin. Fabrics such as cotton and wool are much safer. Curtains, potholders, and dishtowels should also be kept away from heat and flames.

In addition to using cooking appliances safely and being careful around the kitchen, kitchen maintenance is also a critical feature of

 Many fire victims are found in bed with a thin layer of soot over their faces.

fire safety. Keep the stove and oven clean and free of grease buildup. A grease fire is extremely hot and volatile; it can lead to a major fire within a minute. Likewise, the kitchen exhaust fan should be checked at regular intervals to avoid the possibility of an electrical grease and dust fire. Clean crumbs from toaster trays. Don't plug too many electrical appliances into a single outlet. And always check the kitchen each night to be sure that all appliances not in use—from coffeepot to Crockpot—are turned off and unplugged.

A rubber mat placed in front of the stove can help increase traction in case of grease spills; this can save an older person from lying helplessly on the floor next to a raging grease fire. If a grease fire breaks out on a stove, never use water to extinguish the blaze. Cover the fire with a large pot lid, use an approved fire extinguisher, or douse the flames with baking soda. Never use flour to put out a grease fire. Flour explodes. If you can't immediately put out the fire, get out and call the fire department once you are outside.

Finally, regardless of what might have been common practice in days gone by, older people should understand that a stove should never be used to heat the room.

SMOKING

Careless smoking is the number one cause of fire deaths in the United States, and the elderly are just as susceptible as anyone (Figure 8-2). Forgetfulness, the effects of medication, limited mobility, and impaired vision all may put older people at a disadvantage when it comes to smoking. Careless smoking is a major enemy of the elderly, and caution should be exercised accordingly.

Even though most of us associate fires with smoking in bed, most smoking-related fires that cause death actually begin in other furniture, such as a couch or recliner. Naturally, older people should not smoke in bed, but they also should be careful wherever they smoke. Always use large ashtrays that are easy to see and difficult to knock over. Ashtrays should never be dumped straight into the trash. The reduced ability of the elderly to see and smell might lead them to overlook smoldering cigarettes. As an added precaution, keep cigarette butts and ashes separate from regular trash, which may include flammable materials, and clean all ashtrays before bedtime. Matches and lighters should also be handled cautiously. Many older people still use old-fashioned lighters that require handling highly volatile lighter fluid; extra care should be taken when refilling them.

Figure 8-2.

CAUSES OF FIRE DEATHS FOR ELDERLY OVER 70 (ALL OCCUPANCIES)

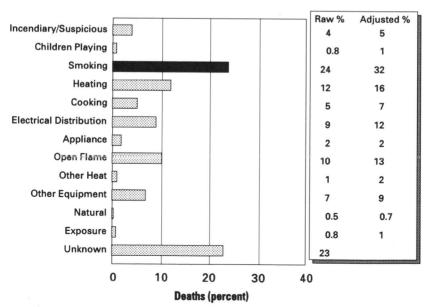

	Raw %	Adjusted %
Incendiary/Suspicious	4	5
Children Playing	0.8	1
Smoking	24	32
Heating	12	16
Cooking	5	7
Electrical Distribution	9	12
Appliance	2	2
Open Flame	10	13
Other Heat	1	2
Other Equipment	7	9
Natural	0.5	0.7
Exposure	0.8	1
Unknown	23	

Deaths (percent)

Source: National Fire Incidents Reporting System

DON'T PATRONIZE, HELP

When we look at an elderly person, we may see a frail old man or woman. But an elderly person looking into the mirror often sees himself as robust and healthy. If there is an elderly person that you care about, be sure to treat him just as you would like to be treated. Never be patronizing or pedantic. Your message will be more effective. And don't assume that the elderly can accomplish everything necessary for fire safety on their own. For example, you or someone you trust should be there when they practice their fire drill. If they can't check their smoke detector, do it for them.

And please don't wait to act. Fire doesn't.

- **Don't** cover the burn with anything except clean dressing.
- **Don't** cover the burn with clothing or absorbent cotton.
- **Don't** remove cloth that sticks to a burn.
- **Don't** break blisters.
- **Don't** apply grease or ointment to severe burns that require medical attention.

10

Fire Safety Away from Home

Most firefighters memorize the number of steps to the exits when they stay at a hotel. People think they're crazy, but they've seen what happens in a fire.

—LIEUTENANT KEVIN BAUM
AUSTIN, TEXAS, FIRE DEPARTMENT

However safe we make our homes, the fact is we aren't always at home. For a large part of the day, our children are in school and we are at work. Every day we travel in cars or use buses, subways, trains, and airplanes. But how many of us think about the issue of fire safety outside the home?

Nonresidential building fires account for about 20 percent of total fire deaths and 40 percent of fire dollar losses annually. Arson is the major cause of deaths, injuries, and dollar loss in commercial properties. Cooking-related accidents are the source of most fires in bars and restaurants, and faulty electrical distribution is responsible for most fires in offices and retail outlets.

HOTELS

Fires at hotels and motels claim fewer lives every year in the United States because the hotel industry has made great strides in improving the safety of their buildings. Most fire injuries are the result of careless smoking, usually in connection with alcohol consumption (see Figure 10-1). But the major cause of fire deaths is arson (Figure 10-2). However the fire is set, the time to make sure you'll get out alive is before a fire ever starts. Planning ahead also helps to avoid panic, and panic can cost you your life.

> When the 1980 Las Vegas MGM Grand fire broke out, the people in the hotel panicked. As the flames engulfed the 26-story structure, more than 3,500 guests and employees were trapped inside. The fire raged for two hours before firefighters could bring it under control. But by then, the carnage was everywhere.
>
> Most victims died of smoke inhalation between the 19th and 24th floors. Hundreds were crushed on stairwells. A thousand guests fled to the roof. Helicopters from a nearby air

✦ **A**t 150°F, the body stops functioning.

Figure 10-1.

CAUSES OF HOTEL / MOTEL FIRE INJURIES

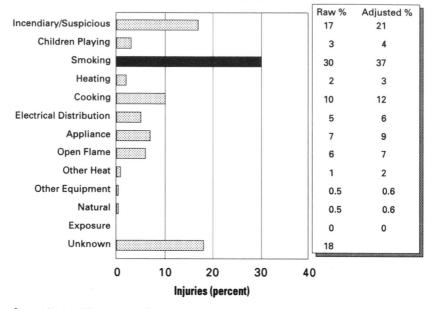

	Raw %	Adjusted %
Incendiary/Suspicious	17	21
Children Playing	3	4
Smoking	30	37
Heating	2	3
Cooking	10	12
Electrical Distribution	5	6
Appliance	7	9
Open Flame	6	7
Other Heat	1	2
Other Equipment	0.5	0.6
Natural	0.5	0.6
Exposure	0	0
Unknown	18	

Injuries (percent)

Source: National Fire Incidents Reporting System

force base hovered over the roof in an attempt to evacuate the stranded guests. Hundreds were saved, but as helicopter pilots watched the desperate guests fighting to scramble onto the rope ladders, they realized that the blades of the choppers were fanning the flames, making the fire burn even faster.

On the street below the high-rise hotel, glass shards rained down on firefighters and onlookers. Two elderly guests jumped to their deaths.

By the time the fire was finally brought under control, 84 people were dead, and 600 more had been seriously injured. Another victim died a few days later.

You can begin your fire safety preparation when you (or your travel agent) make the reservations. Ask if the hotel has smoke detectors in each room. Are there sprinklers? A simple question such as ''What kind of fire safety precautions are in place at the

Figure 10-2.
CAUSES OF HOTEL / MOTEL FIRE DEATHS

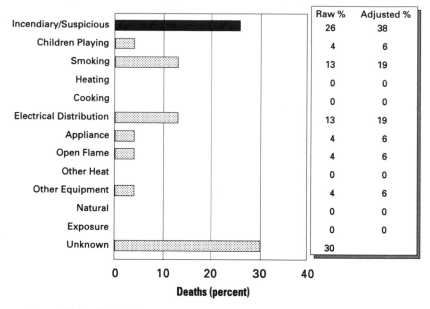

Source: National Fire Incidents Reporting System

hotel?'' may reveal just how seriously the hotel takes the subject of fire safety. Remember, you will be spending the night under the same roof with dozens, if not hundreds, of other people, all of them strangers.

Carry a few fire safety items in a survival kit. The National Safety Council recommends a flashlight, some duct tape for sealing out smoke around doors and windows, and a portable smoke detector.

When you check in, ask the hotel manager or desk clerk what to do in case of fire, and find out where the exits are. It's at least as important as locating the ice machine, an item most hotels are only too eager to point out.

When you arrive on your floor, don't just find out where the exits are, determine how you'd open an exit door and, if you can, check the stairwell to see if there are emergency lights. If you were forced to exit, you might be crawling, so take note of the hallway features, such as the number of doors between your room and the exit.

Once inside your room, take a few minutes to devise an escape plan. Do the windows open? If they don't, you may not be able to smash them open in case of an emergency. At a hotel fire in Ohio, a number of guests on the first and second floors died because they couldn't open the windows. The windows, which were made of safety glass, did not even break when the guests tried to smash them with furniture. You should consider breaking the window only as a last resort. A large hole in a window, or a window that is opened too wide, acts to draw smoke *into* your room through the door and vents. Also, if smoke begins to blow into the room from outside, you won't be able to block it out.

If the windows do open, decide whether or not it would be feasible for you to escape unassisted via the window without jumping. Jumping out of windows has led to many unnecessary deaths; it is rarely worth the risk.

In case of fire, you may have to crawl to the exit, so know your room layout. Keep the room key beside your bed. If you leave your room and find that the exits are blocked, you will need the key to get back inside.

If you hear a fire alarm when you are in your room, call the front desk and tell the clerk. Don't take it for granted that the management already knows.

Remember that your hotel door provides a strong defense against a fire if it is closed. Always touch the door or doorknob before you open the door to determine if the fire is close to your room. If the door is hot, don't open it. Use your phone to call for help. If your window opens, hang a towel or sheet out the window to signal for help.

Fill the bathtub with water. Soak some towels and stuff them around the edge of the door to prevent smoke from seeping into the room. Also cover the vents if smoke is entering through them. Duct tape is handy here, because it can be used to tape a magazine or newspaper over the vent. Any wet item—paper, clothes, bedding— can seal out smoke. If necessary, the water can be used to cool down the walls. Use your ice bucket.

If the room becomes filled with smoke, soak your clothing and place a wet towel over your head. Also prepare a small triangle of wet cloth for your face. Use it to breathe through and filter out smoke. Open the window wide enough to stick your head outside.

If the door is not hot, open it slowly, but be prepared to close it again if the hallway is full of smoke. If the corridor is clear of smoke, close your room door behind you and walk to the exit. Take your keys. Never take the elevator in case of a fire.

If you see someone going the wrong way, try to get him or her to follow you. However, don't expect anyone caught in a fire to act rationally. Most people aren't prepared for a fire, so they panic. One of the few survivors of the catastrophic Happy Land Social Club fire in New York City reported that he had shouted to the crowd, ''If you want to survive, follow me.'' No one did.

On the stairs, remember to hold the railing. It will keep you from being knocked down if people in the stairwell stampede and try to push past you.

One of the safest alternatives in a high-rise hotel room, however, is to stay put. Block the smoke from entering your room, call the fire department to give them your location, and wait for help. Most high-rise rooms are designed to hold back smoke if the door stays closed. Don't walk into danger if you are safe where you are. Concrete floors and steel doors offer protection.

If the fire is in your room, don't stand up. The heat and poisonous gases at head level can kill you. Crawl to the door. Test it to see if it is hot. If it is safe to exit, leave the room and close the door. If the fire is confined to your room alone, closing the door will prevent the fire from spreading and could save countless lives. Wake your neighbors, sound the nearest fire alarm, and call the front desk on the nearest phone to notify them of the fire.

AUTOMOBILES

It probably never occurs to you when you ride in your car that you might be traveling in a firetrap. But every year hundreds of Americans die in automobile fires. Despite the mortality rate, few national automobile groups have studied this problem, which clearly requires more attention from drivers, manufacturers, and auto associations alike. (See also Chapter 3.)

Because newer model cars are made with a great deal of plastic, they burn more quickly and more intensely than older models. As a safety measure, the makers have installed fire walls between the engine and passenger compartment and between the trunk and passenger compartment to contain fires. However, gaps created by such things as the steering column can allow a fire to penetrate into the passenger area.

Most automobile fire deaths occur as the result of a collision. Therefore, if you're unfortunate enough to be involved in an automobile accident, get away from the car as quickly as possible. First aid experts advise that accident victims with back or neck injuries should never be moved without the aid of a health professional, but if you can move safely, get yourself and the other passengers away

 Between one-tenth and one-third of all smoke detectors don't function because the batteries are dead or have been removed.

from the car. Pay special attention to children locked into car seats and anyone else who appears unable to extricate herself from the wreckage.

Inside the passenger compartment, most automobiles are made of materials designed to self-extinguish. Carpeting, upholstery, and dashboard are all made of material that will not support combustion. Although this material will burn and char, it is rare that it will explode into flames the way furniture in your home might.

Keep a small fire extinguisher beneath the dashboard to help put out small fires. But unless you can put it out within 30 seconds, don't attempt to extinguish the blaze.

Never attempt to put out a fire under the hood unless you are there when it begins and the fire is small. Electrical fires, while uncommon, are dangerous and can cause explosions. Fortunately, there is little fire load—that is, items that combust easily—beneath the hood.

If you see flames coming from under the hood, get away from the car. If you have time before leaving, turn off the ignition.

If you have a camper, a trailer, or any other vehicle with sleeping accommodations, you should always have a fire extinguisher, just as you should have one in your house.

The most dangerous car fires are those involving gasoline, which is extraordinarily volatile. Never try to fight a gas fire in your car. Gasoline has a flash point of −45°F. A tiny spark can ignite it. In

 A multiple fire death (three or more people), not including firefighting personnel, has never been reported in a building equipped with a working sprinkler system.

case of a fire in the area of the gas tank, get as far away from the vehicle as you can; leave the firefighting to professionals.

Never carry gas in the trunk of your car, even in an approved container. The potential for disaster is enormous. The advantages of having spare gasoline are far outweighed by the disadvantages of carrying a powerful explosive in the same vehicle with your family.

MASS TRANSPORTATION

In mass transit fires, as at home, it's not the flames that injure and kill, it's the smoke and fumes. Although aircraft and other transportation manufacturers sometimes use fire-resistant and nontoxic materials in construction, all too often they do not. If you see a fire in the bus, plane, train, or ship in which you are traveling, stay low to avoid the poisonous gases that accompany a blaze.

> When a small fire broke out in a New York City subway tunnel between Manhattan and Brooklyn in late 1990, the Transit Authority reported only "a light smoke condition." But when the heavy smoke that choked the tunnel finally cleared, two passengers were dead and 150 more were injured.

Whenever you travel by any form of mass transit, note the location of the exits and read posted evacuation plans when you board. Have an escape plan. Take time to memorize the procedures to follow in case of an emergency. Allowing a few minutes to familiarize yourself with these details at the beginning of your trip may save your life later . . . and allow you to travel with a bit more peace of mind.

If you are traveling with a small child, show the passenger next to you how to unbuckle the baby's safety belt or safety seat. In case you're incapacitated, someone else will be able to rescue the child.

AIRPLANES

There are few things more terrifying than an airplane fire. In addition to the fear that any fire can engender, an aircraft fire also means being trapped in a small, enclosed space with many other people. Because there are no openings to let in the fresh air, the dangers from smoke and poisonous gases are even greater than in other fires.

> Flames and smoke poured through a USAir jet on February 1, 1991, within the first two minutes after it crashed on the runway at Los Angeles International Airport. Twenty-two people were killed. The panic that ensued shocked survivors, who reported that hysterical passengers had clawed their way over others in a stampede to get to an exit.

Because of bans on smoking on U.S. domestic flights of under six hours, some foolish people resort to smoking in the lavatories, thereafter discarding their cigarette butts in the wastebaskets. As a result, wastebasket fires start in airplane lavatories. So serious is the potential for fire that smoking in the restrooms and tampering with restroom smoke detectors are prohibited by federal law.

Many of us ignore—or at best give short shrift to—the safety lecture given by flight attendants after takeoff. But if you should have the misfortune to be trapped in a burning airplane, the panic and commotion around you may make it impossible to hear the emergency instructions of airline personnel (who are well trained to handle these situations). If you know what to do in advance, you have a far better chance of surviving and may help others to survive as well.

AIRPLANE SAFETY GUIDELINES
- After boarding, listen to the flight attendant's safety instructions and read the emergency procedures checklist.

- You should know where all the exits are, how to reach them in an emergency, and how to use them. Check to see which exit is closest to your seat.
- If you are not seated next to an emergency exit, count the number of seats between you and the exit. Could you reach it while crawling on your hands and knees?
- In an emergency, follow the white lights along the aisles until you reach the red lights, which indicate an exit.
- Know the procedures for opening the emergency exit.
- When some emergency doors open, a slide inflates to allow people to exit. The procedure is to jump into the slide in a seated position with your arms crossed and legs extended. Don't take time to sit down on the slide—just jump. The precious seconds you waste sitting down may cost those at the end of the line their lives. If you're wearing high heels, take them off; the point of the heel might tear the slide.
- If you see a small fire, notify a flight attendant quickly and calmly. If you have immediate access to a fire extinguisher and know how to use it, aim the nozzle at the base of the fire and spray using side-to-side motions. Fire extinguishers have a limited amount of suppressant, so aim carefully. The extinguisher may run out before you get a second chance.

Statistically, airline travel is one of the safest modes of transportation, so it's highly unlikely that you will ever be faced with an airplane fire. However remote the chance, it's always best to be prepared. In these highly volatile situations, a little preparation can make the difference between life and death.

 Most fire fatalities occur within the first five minutes after the fire starts.

CRUISE SHIPS

Cruise ships are an increasingly popular venue for vacations. In 1987, three and a half million Americans were passengers on cruises. But ships can also be hazardous. As the Marine Safety Council stated in 1990, "Fire and explosion pose a continuing threat to life and property at sea, especially when smoke and toxic gases get out of control aboard ship."

Navigating the corridors of these floating resorts is difficult enough during daylight hours under normal conditions. Imagine what it would be like in an emergency. To protect yourself, listen carefully to safety messages when you first come aboard the ship. Know your exits. In an emergency, pay close attention to the crew; if disaster strikes be prepared to use the lifeboats.

SCHOOLS AND CAMPUSES

Fire safety is an essential part of your child's education. Fortunately, many school districts take fire safety very seriously. In many families, the children know more about the subject than their parents. But be sure: Does your child know how to get out if a fire occurs at her school? During parent-teacher meetings, ask about fire safety in the class. Not only will it make you feel better, it will also remind teachers of its importance.

About one out of five school fires originates in a restroom or locker room. Some of them can be traced to a carelessly discarded cigarette; others are simply listed as "of suspicious origin." In fact, as many as half of all school fires are of suspicious origin. Kids who set wastebaskets and dumpsters on fire only intend to cause a disruption; usually, they don't see the potential for death and injury.

When your son or daughter goes to college, he or she encounters a new scenario rife with the danger of fire: Students drink and smoke—a surefire combination for danger. Therefore, it's important that their living quarters are equipped with sufficient exits, smoke detectors, and sprinklers, and that they are otherwise adequately protected from fire. Forty percent of fires at sleep-away institutions begin in the sleeping area. Ask school authorities about fire safety before your child goes away to college or university.

AT WORK

Figure 10-3 shows the causes of fires in stores and offices. Arson and electrical distribution rank high on the list. The rules of home safety also apply to the workplace. You need to know how to find

Figure 10-3.

CAUSES OF STORE AND OFFICE FIRES

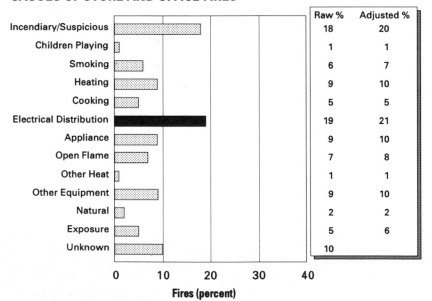

	Raw %	Adjusted %
Incendiary/Suspicious	18	20
Children Playing	1	1
Smoking	6	7
Heating	9	10
Cooking	5	5
Electrical Distribution	19	21
Appliance	9	10
Open Flame	7	8
Other Heat	1	1
Other Equipment	9	10
Natural	2	2
Exposure	5	6
Unknown	10	

Fires (percent)

Source: National Fire Incidents Reporting System

your way out. You need to know where fire extinguishers are and how to use them. And you need to know how to notify the fire department in the event of an emergency.

Learn the procedures to follow in case of fire. Know who the fire warden is for your floor—and there should be a fire warden on every floor in every business establishment. Find out what kind of alarm will sound if there's a fire on your floor; in many buildings, a different alarm sounds when the fire is on another floor.

High-rise workplaces are dangerous too, especially when there is no sprinkler system. Sprinklers should be in every high-rise building in America.

A dramatic example of what can happen without sprinklers occurred when a fire broke out on the 12th floor of the First Interstate Bank Building in downtown Los Angeles at 10 P.M. in May 1988. The first security guard to hear the automatic smoke alarm took an elevator to the 12th floor to investigate. When the elevator doors opened, he was killed instantly by the billowing smoke. Around the same time, the fire burst through the windows and crept up to the 13th floor. By this time—four minutes after the start of the fire—the fire department had arrived. Trudging up 13 floors with their equipment, firefighters fought the blaze for four hours. Because it was nighttime, only three people died, far fewer than might have been killed if the fire had occurred during the day. This single fire cost $50 million. It required months of work to reconstruct the building.

 Doors are one of the best pieces of fire-fighting equipment. Always close the door behind you when you exit a burning room.

A good rule of thumb is to stay put if you are in a closed area that can be sealed away from the fire. If you are directly threatened by a fire, leave the floor and proceed downward on the stairs to escape. Avoid going to the roof except as a last resort.

WHERE PEOPLE GATHER

Any other place where people gather—social clubs, churches, restaurants—should have basic fire safety equipment, including fire alarms, fire extinguishers, smoke detectors, emergency stairwells, and clearly marked exits. If you visit a place frequently, you should become familiar with its fire safety features and draft an escape plan in your mind. Since approximately one of four fires in public assembly areas is cooking-related, safety in the kitchen area is particularly important.

For organizers in charge of choosing a meeting place, safety should be a top priority. Rooms should have the following ratio of exits to number of participants: at least two exits for the first 300 people, three exits for groups up to 1,000, and an additional exit for each 500 people.

11

Firefighting Equipment That Can Save Your Life

The fire loss in this country in residential occupancies is catastrophic. Manual firefighting methods are not the answer. The way to attack the problem is to limit the fire growth where it occurs in dwellings. We have the technology to do that.

—ORDINANCE NO. 745, ADOPTED 1969
SAN CLEMENTE, CALIFORNIA, CITY COUNCIL

Fires are one of the few social problems for which there are readymade technological solutions. Although the human fac-

127

tor is the most critical element in fire safety, the warning and suppression devices produced in the past few decades have proven to be highly effective. Among the most important categories of fire warning and firefighting equipment are smoke detectors, fire extinguishers, and sprinklers.

SMOKE DETECTORS

Probably nothing has done more to save lives from fire than the widespread introduction of smoke detectors in residences, the workplace, and other areas where people gather. Developed and perfected in the 1960s, smoke detectors began to be installed widely in the 1970s and 80s. Inexpensive, simple to install, and easy to maintain, smoke detectors have dramatically cut the loss of life in homes where they have been installed. About 90 percent of all residential fire deaths and 80 percent of all residential fire injuries occur in buildings without working smoke detectors. This section will discuss how the systems work, how to install them, where they should be placed, and what maintenance they require.

According to the U.S. Fire Administration, people who live in homes with working smoke detectors are twice as likely to survive a fire as people who live in homes without detectors. Because they warn you before it's too late to escape, smoke detectors are known as the "first line of defense" in the event of a fire. Smoke detectors can neither prevent nor stop a fire, but they do give you precious seconds to get out. And that may be all that's needed to survive in case of a fire.

One of the most important things to remember about smoke detectors is that they operate only when they have a working power source. Even though most American homes now have smoke detectors, as many as one-third to one-half of those detectors are useless because the battery has been removed or is dead. If your smoke detector is powered by your home's AC current, it's important that you have a reliable energy supply. Areas that experience frequent power failures should not rely solely on AC-powered detectors. Use AC-powered detectors that have a battery backup or use both AC- and battery-powered detectors.

Ionization Detectors

There are two main types of smoke detectors—ionization and photoelectric. First we will examine ionization detectors. This type is the most common, about 90 percent of all detectors.

Ionization smoke detectors use a minute bit of radioactive material to create a field of ions that carries a flow of electrical current inside the smoke detector's chamber—the area behind the plastic dome of the detector. When enough particles of smoke enter the chamber, the electrical current is interrupted, tripping a circuit that sets off the loud, high-pitched squeal of the alarm (see Figure 11-1).

Figure 11-1.
IONIZATION DETECTOR

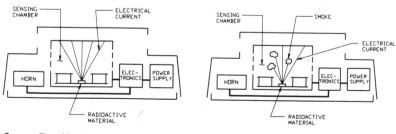

Source: First Alert

The radioactive material contained in ionization smoke detectors is no cause for concern. The radioactive source itself is carefully shielded. According to the U.S. Nuclear Regulatory Commission, someone who is in physical contact with an ionization-type smoke detector for eight hours a day for an entire year receives only about one-tenth the radiation a person receives when flying round-trip between New York and California.

Smoke particles don't have to be very large to activate a smoke detector. The ionization mechanism is so sensitive that even particles invisible to the naked eye can be detected.

A hot, blazing fire produces many more smoke particles than a slow-burning, smoldering fire. In hot blazes, the ionization detectors could be expected to detect a fire more quickly than the photoelectric type, although, according to *Consumer Reports,* the time difference would be very small.

Because it is essential that the detector be able to recognize particles of smoke that enter the chamber, the chamber must be kept free of dust and debris, such as insects. Since 1986, Underwriters Laboratories has mandated that smoke detectors include screens to keep out insects.

Photoelectric Detectors

The other main type of smoke detector uses the same kind of surveillance system that your eyes use to detect smoke—they ''see'' it. Photoelectric detectors use a small beam of light aimed at a dark

Every 15 seconds a fire department responds to a fire alarm somewhere in the United States.

corner in the light-tight chamber of the smoke detector. As long as the beam is not reflected, the detector stays quiet.

When particles of smoke are carried into the air, however, some enter the light-tight chamber. When these particles get in front of the light beam, they scatter the light and reflect it onto a light-sensitive photocell. When enough light is bounced onto the photocell, an electrical current is created that activates the alarm (see Figure 11-2).

Because light-sensitive detectors have to "see" the particles of

Figure 11-2.

PHOTOELECTRIC DETECTOR

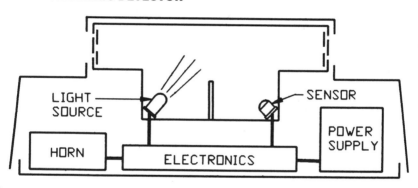

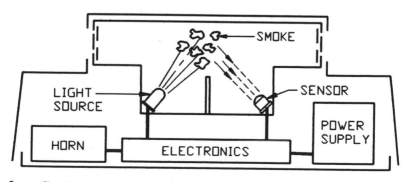

Source: First Alert

smoke, they react more quickly to larger particles, the kind released in slow, smoldering fires, such as those created by lighted cigarettes dropped between furniture cushions.

Be sure to keep photoelectric detectors at least five feet away from fluorescent light fixtures. Fluorescent lights create an electrical "noise" that can fool photoelectric detectors and set off nuisance alarms.

The U.S. Consumer Product Safety Commission points out that many household fires produce both large and small particles of smoke. Either type of detector is a valuable component of fire safety; however, to cover all bases, it's a good idea to install both types. (And always look for the UL label.)

Whichever type you choose, get a smoke detector and install it without delay. Every night you and your family spend without this simple, low-cost protection from fire represents an unacceptable risk.

Heat Detectors

Some smoke detectors include heat-sensitive devices that rely not on smoke, but on increased temperatures alone to set off an alarm. These detectors usually contain a piece of metal that has been specially formulated to melt or bend when it gets hot. If the heat detector is built into the smoke detector, it sets off the detector's alarm. If the heat detector is a separate unit, it is usually hooked up to a central alarm system that is set off by high temperatures around the heat detector.

Heat detectors work only when they are close enough to a fire to sense the heat. This feature is particularly useful in areas such as a garage or kitchen, where smoke detectors might be fooled by smoke even when there is no fire. Thus, it can cut down on nuisance alarms. (However, nuisance alarms are not as frequent or troublesome as you might think. According to *Consumer Reports,* a public opinion survey revealed that people who *don't* have smoke detectors are twice as likely to worry about nuisance alarms as people who do!)

Nuisance alarms aside, never use a heat detector as a substitute for a smoke detector. Remember, most people are killed by smoke, not by the flames of a fire. If a smoldering fire is producing poisonous gases and fumes, a heat detector will not act in time to warn you of the real danger you face.

Power Sources for Smoke Detectors

There are two main sources of power for a smoke detector: batteries and household current.

Battery-powered detectors are usually easier to install. About all that's required is attaching the detector to the wall or ceiling and then replacing the battery as necessary. Most batteries last about one year, and many detectors are designed to set off a warning "beep" when the power begins to fail. It is critical that batteries be replaced at the first warning of failure and that they be checked twice a year. A good time to check is in the spring and fall, when the clocks are changed to and from Daylight Savings Time.

If you decide to use household current to power your smoke detectors, you can avoid the hassle of replacing your batteries, but there are several disadvantages. For one thing, the installation of

 In the United States, there is a structural fire every 45 seconds, a residential fire every 60 seconds, and a motor vehicle fire every 72 seconds.

the unit itself may be more difficult and often requires the help of a professional electrician.

AC-powered detectors that can be plugged in (no longer in common use) should never be connected to an outlet by a long extension cord. For one thing, this arrangement puts an additional plug between the detector and the power source. If the secondary connection becomes unplugged, it may go unnoticed. And an unplugged detector is as worthless as one with dead batteries.

If an electrician is called in, have him or her simply tie the detector directly into the home's wiring, even though this type of installation can be costly and time-consuming. It's good to wire the detector into a line that will also supply power to another appliance, such as a lamp, so that if the power supply for that line is interrupted it will be easier to detect.

Another drawback to AC-powered detectors is that if the household power fails, so does the detector. For this reason, some AC-powered detectors have standby emergency batteries for backup. But don't take it for granted that the detector you are purchasing has a standby power supply. If it does, remember to check the battery regularly, just as you would for any battery-powered detector.

Where to Install Smoke Detectors

You can never have too many smoke detectors, but even one offers far more protection than none. The U.S. Fire Administration estimates that a single smoke detector will allow you three minutes to escape a fire about 35 percent of the time. Two detectors, however,

About 15 percent of all fire fatalities occur in motor vehicles.

will provide three minutes of escape time almost 90 percent of the time. In addition, two detectors will allow for the possibility of backup in an emergency, since it's far more unlikely that both detectors will be malfunctioning than just one.

At the very minimum, you should have one smoke detector for every floor in your home. A detector located on a different floor from the fire will take several additional minutes to go off, longer than a detector located on the same floor as the fire. Furthermore, just as closed doors can keep the smoke away from you, they also keep smoke away from detectors. If you sleep with your door closed, you should install smoke detectors both outside and inside your bedroom—one to warn the rest of the family of a fire inside your room and one to warn you of a fire in other parts of the house. This is particularly important if you or any member of the family smokes in bed—even if he or she does so infrequently. The presence of space heaters in a bedroom also calls for the installation of a smoke detector in that room.

Because the detector has to be able to wake up the household in case of a fire, it's best to locate the detector as close as possible to the sleeping area. The U.S. Consumer Product Safety Commission recommends that the detector be placed "between the bedrooms and the rest of the house, but closer to the bedrooms" (see Figure 11-3).

Positioning the Smoke Detector

The user's manual that comes with your smoke detector should provide you with complete instructions on how to install it, including the exact position on the wall or ceiling for optimal use. It might be wise to avoid buying a detector that does not have clear and full instructions.

Under most circumstances, smoke detectors should be installed

Figure 11-3.
CORRECT AND INCORRECT POSITIONING FOR SMOKE DETECTORS

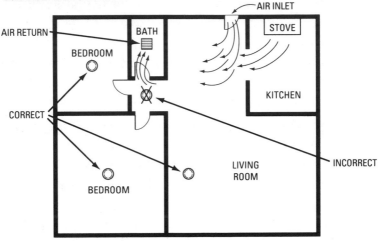

Source: First Alert

Figure 11-4.
POSITIONING THE SMOKE DETECTOR

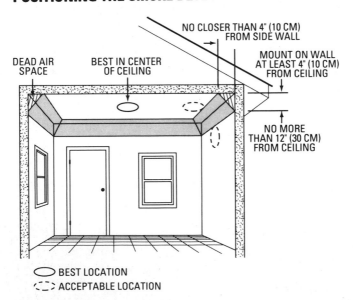

Source: First Alert

on the ceiling. If that isn't possible, use the wall, between six and 12 inches from the ceiling. Positioning the detector high on the wall keeps it out of the way of curious children and most activities in the home. Also, it takes advantage of the movement of smoke, which rises. For the best locations and those to avoid, see Figure 11-4.

One of the worst places to install the detector is at the exact point where the ceiling and wall meet. This place has proven to be a "dead air" area of a room, just out of reach of the roll and puff of smoke and fumes. Another spot to avoid is directly in front of an air vent. Because the vent may cause a continuous sweep of "clean" air to pass through the detector, it may prevent smoke from reaching the detector, thus rendering it useless.

Just as clean air is a hazard to the proper function of detectors, so is dirty air. Dust and debris in the air can cause nuisance alarms or clog the vents into the alarm, preventing it from detecting smoke.

Don't place detectors within 20 feet of a water heater, furnace, or gas space heater. If you must locate a smoke detector in an area within that range, use a photoelectric detector. Try not to place a detector near a bathroom, since the water particles from shower and bath steam may cause the alarm to sound. Keep the detector 10 feet away from bathroom doors. Other damp areas, such as wet basements with severe condensation problems, should also be avoided.

Avoid placing smoke detectors against outside walls or ceilings that are poorly insulated. Exposure to heat or cold may create a thermal barrier that keeps smoke away from the wall or ceiling and

 Vehicle fires in the United States cause about $170 million worth of damage annually.

the detector. These conditions are most common in older houses, including mobile homes. If you live in a poorly insulated home, place the detector on an inside wall and avoid the ceiling altogether.

Finally, remember that smoke detectors are not toys. Children should not be permitted to set off the alarms on purpose. Excessive testing will drain the battery, leaving the detector useless in an actual emergency.

SPRINKLERS

Henry Parmalee invented sprinklers in 1874 to protect his piano factory from fire. Following a series of devastating fires that brought heavy loss of lives and property, the textile mills of New England also began installing them as a safety measure. Now, over a hundred years later, sprinklers have become the standard by which fire safety is measured.

Sprinklers save lives, but because of costs—about 90 cents to $1.90 per square foot in new construction and 50 percent more for retrofit—most single-family residences don't have them. But that is changing. The vastly increased efficiency of these systems, lowered insurance costs (from five to 15 percent less), and the development of more fire-resistant structural components have made sprinkler installation a more and more attractive option. Some industry experts estimate that sprinkler systems installed at the time of construction add less than one percent to total construction costs. Today, some communities—such as Greenburg, New York; San Clemente, California; and Cobb County, Georgia—have passed laws that encourage single-family houses to have sprinkler systems.

Sprinklers are highly effective. No multiple fire death has ever been reported in an area of a building with a working sprinkler system. That statistic doesn't include firefighter deaths or deaths from explosions. According to the National Fire Sprinkler Association, New York City—which requires sprinklers in all high-rise buildings—has a success rate of over 98 percent for fire suppression in buildings equipped with sprinklers.

How Sprinklers Work

Sprinklers are constructed of a series of interconnected pipes carrying pressurized water and a number of individually heat-activated sprinkler heads. When the temperature reaches 165–175°F, the sprinkler releases a spray of water. The fear that sprinklers can discharge accidentally is largely unfounded. It's estimated that the chances of such an event are less than one in 16 million, according to the National Fire Sprinkler Association.

Some people worry about the water damage from sprinklers. Yet the water damage from a "sprinkled" fire is far less severe (from ten to a hundred times less severe) than the damage caused by the intervention of fire departments. Also, it's important to note that when one sprinkler goes off, the rest do not. Only sprinklers exposed to high temperature are activated.

Although the cost of sprinkler systems and the expense of their installation are obvious drawbacks, sprinklers still offer the best solution for dealing with difficult fire safety problems, such as homes with elderly, very young, or disabled residents.

FIRE EXTINGUISHERS

Fire extinguishers are pressurized tanks that release a steady spray of chemicals or water to help put out a fire. Knowing when *not* to use fire extinguishers can be as important as knowing when to use them. According to the New York State Office of Fire Prevention and Control, about one-fourth of all civilian fire-related injuries occur when the victim attempts to control or extinguish the fire. But knowing *how* to use them is most important of all.

Extinguishers can keep a small fire from getting bigger and spreading. They can also buy time for you and your family to escape. But fire extinguishers are no substitute for the fire department. Never attempt to put out a large fire with a fire extinguisher. Use your time to get out. Only use a fire extinguisher when you have your back to an exit in case the small fire you're fighting spreads.

How Fire Extinguishers Work

Extinguishers work by removing one of the three necessary components—fuel, oxygen, and heat—fire needs to burn. Extinguishers either cool down the fire, removing heat, or use a chemical that smothers the fire. The three components of fire combine in a chemical reaction. Sometimes a fire extinguisher works to block the chemical reaction itself.

Extinguishers are designed to work on specific fires. There are three major types of extinguishers—Class A, Class BC, and Class ABC.

Class A extinguishers work on the types of fires associated with such flammable materials as wood, paper, clothing, furniture, plastics, and so forth. These types of combustibles form the basis of most fires in the home outside of the kitchen. For these fires, the

 Out of every 100 cases of arson, 99 go unresolved.

ingredient in Class A extinguishers—monomodium phosphate—works best to suppress the blaze.

When a fire is fueled by flammable liquids—including kerosene, gasoline, paints and oils, and kitchen grease—or involves electricity—such as electrical equipment and wiring—use a Class BC extinguisher. These work well in the kitchen because they contain a dry chemical (sodium bicarbonate) that will not corrode appliances or kitchen enamel. (Note: You can use a Class A fire extinguisher on electric and grease fires, but its main ingredient, monomodium phosphate, is corrosive.) A Class BC extinguisher can also be used to put out small electrical or grease fires in cars (but only attempt to extinguish an automobile engine fire if you are there when it begins and it is small).

Class BC extinguishers can be used on fires that are not electrical or grease- or oil-based, such as wood, cloth, and furniture. However, this extinguisher is not as effective on these types of fires as a Class A extinguisher.

Class ABC extinguishers can be used on most types of household fires. Its one disadvantage is the corrosiveness of its main ingredient, monomodium phosphate, on kitchen appliances.

Using Fire Extinguishers

Every able-bodied member of the family should know how to operate fire extinguishers safely. Quality fire extinguishers should come with explicit instructions for operation enclosed in the package.

Pyromaniacs—those with a pathological need to set fires—account for only five percent of all arson cases.

Figure 11-5.

OPERATING A FIRE EXTINGUISHER

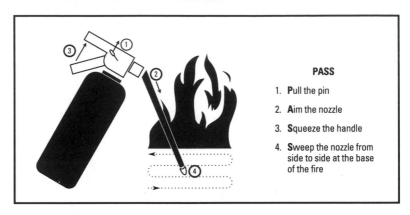

PASS

1. **P**ull the pin
2. **A**im the nozzle
3. **S**queeze the handle
4. **S**weep the nozzle from side to side at the base of the fire

Source: New York Office of Fire Prevention and Control

The New York Office of Fire Prevention and Control uses the acronym "PASS" for the basics of fire extinguisher operation. PASS stands for Pull, Aim, Squeeze, Sweep. For an explanation of how to use a fire extinguisher, see Figure 11-5.

Fire extinguishers should be easily accessible, not in a place that is likely to be between you and the fire—for example, not above the stove, but beside it; not behind the workbench, but in front of it.

Remind children that fire extinguishers are not toys; a partially discharged extinguisher is no better than an empty one. Be sure that extinguishers are not corroded or leaky and have not been subjected to tampering. Above all, learn how to use the extinguisher *before* you need it. Once you spot a fire, you only have 30 seconds to put it out. You no longer have time to study the instructions.

12

Making Fire Prevention Work

For the longest time, we've been our own worst enemy. There are other ways to fight fire besides putting them out. It used to be that the bigger the fire truck, the better you are. Over the next 10 years, you'll see a big turnaround. Fire prevention is where it's at.

—COLONEL H. LEWIS YOUNG
COBB COUNTY, GEORGIA, FIRE AND EMERGENCY SERVICES

lmost every fire department in the United States has some
form of fire prevention program, but most of them are poorly

funded and receive little support from city officials. In fact, fire officials know that a successful prevention program can actually hurt their budgets. When prevention programs are implemented, fire incidence decreases. When fire incidence decreases, budgets are cut and fire halls are closed.

When it comes to spending, city officials are painfully aware that prevention programs don't have nearly the political cachet that a new fire hall or fire engine has.

As the work of fire researcher Phil Schaenman of TriData Corporation has shown, the thing that separates the United States from the rest of the industrialized world is our attitude toward fire education. Even though the nation as a whole still lags far behind other countries, those communities that have focused their efforts on fire prevention programs have been rewarded with a steadily declining rate of fire deaths. But the U.S. fire death rate is still obscenely high. Much more remains to be done. Figures 12-1 and 12-2 show the number of deaths per million population, by state.

This chapter examines three communities that have made outstanding progress in fire education: Austin, Texas; Portland, Oregon; and Cobb County, Georgia. All of these communities have tackled their fire problems head on with intensive public education campaigns. No two cities are alike; each has its own set of unique circumstances. But there are lessons here that can benefit every town.

 Fires are one of the few social problems for which widely available solutions exist.

Figure 12-1.

FIRE DEATHS BY STATE

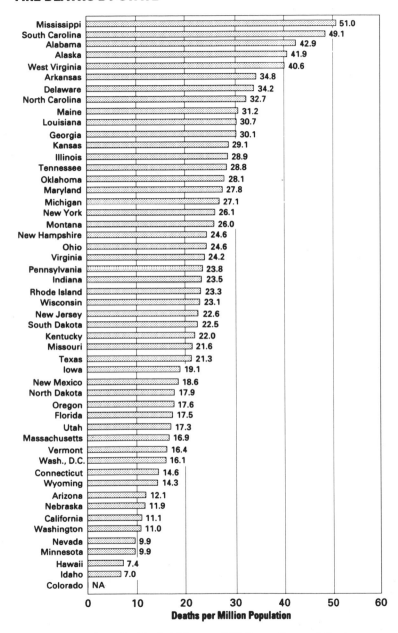

State	Deaths per Million Population
Mississippi	51.0
South Carolina	49.1
Alabama	42.9
Alaska	41.9
West Virginia	40.6
Arkansas	34.8
Delaware	34.2
North Carolina	32.7
Maine	31.2
Louisiana	30.7
Georgia	30.1
Kansas	29.1
Illinois	28.9
Tennessee	28.8
Oklahoma	28.1
Maryland	27.8
Michigan	27.1
New York	26.1
Montana	26.0
New Hampshire	24.6
Ohio	24.6
Virginia	24.2
Pennsylvania	23.8
Indiana	23.5
Rhode Island	23.3
Wisconsin	23.1
New Jersey	22.6
South Dakota	22.5
Kentucky	22.0
Missouri	21.6
Texas	21.3
Iowa	19.1
New Mexico	18.6
North Dakota	17.9
Oregon	17.6
Florida	17.5
Utah	17.3
Massachusetts	16.9
Vermont	16.4
Wash., D.C.	16.1
Connecticut	14.6
Wyoming	14.3
Arizona	12.1
Nebraska	11.9
California	11.1
Washington	11.0
Nevada	9.9
Minnesota	9.9
Hawaii	7.4
Idaho	7.0
Colorado	NA

Deaths per Million Population

Source: Primarily State Fire Marshal Offices and U.S. Census (for populations)

Figure 12-2.

DISTRIBUTION OF FIRE DEATHS BY STATE

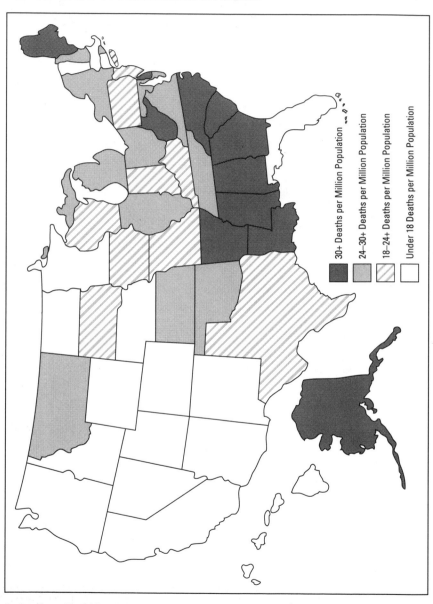

30+ Deaths per Million Population

24–30+ Deaths per Million Population

18–24+ Deaths per Million Population

Under 18 Deaths per Million Population

Source: State Fire Marshals

PORTLAND, OREGON:
SNUFFING OUT ARSON

Portland consistently ranks as one of the nation's most beautiful and livable cities. It is an urban jewel set on the banks of the Willamette and Columbia rivers and framed by the Cascade Range.

In the late 1960s, when many of the nation's inner cities were crumbling, downtown Portland underwent a renaissance. The revitalized downtown features an advanced mass transit system, stunning office buildings, and an extensive network of parks.

Portland is known as a city of neighborhoods, but in one district bordering the downtown area, known as "Northwest," arson was a growing problem. Whereas about one out of five fires in Portland overall was a result of arson, in Northwest the ratio was one in three. Between 1981 and 1986, 175 fires were set. Dollar loss was in excess of $800,000 and climbing annually.

With grants from the U.S. Fire Administration and the Portland Police Department, the Northwest District Association and Neighbors West/Northwest, two community groups, mobilized to fight the arson problem. Studying trends in the neighborhood, the prevention group determined that most fires occurred in the large apartment complexes that typified the district. Almost 90 percent of the district's residents live in apartment houses. On average, their incomes are about half that of other Portlanders.

The group developed a plan that called for educating apartment managers, owners, and residents about arson. They used the grant from the police department to beef up security at one apartment

 One of five fire deaths occurs outside the home.

complex that had been a repeat target for arsonists. They also organized two four-hour seminars to teach the building managers how to prevent arson. The most significant piece of advice, according to James Hussey, the prevention project's coordinator, is to eliminate the fuel that arsonists need to do their dirty work. ''We always say that arson is an opportunity crime,'' says Hussey. ''Arsonists don't carry burnables. They look for them.''

Besides sponsoring the seminars, the group also created a training manual that teaches basic facts about arson, including fires set by children, pyromania, vandalism, revenge, and arson for profit. The booklets also included advice on smoke detectors, how to use a fire extinguisher, and how to organize a neighborhood arson watch.

The results were impressive. In fiscal year 1986–87, 32 arson fires caused almost $30,000 in damage. One year after the start of the program, the number of fires dropped to 11, and dollar loss declined to under $4,000.

AUSTIN, TEXAS: A FIRE-SMART CITY

Austin, the capital of Texas, is a progressive town of approximately 465,000 residents representing a diverse ethnic and cultural mix. It's a city that prizes its educational institutions, which include the University of Texas, Huston-Tillotson College, and St. Edward's University. Austin claims that it is the most educated city of its size in the country.

When the city began an effort to make education the cornerstone

 About 50 people die every year in hotel and motel fires in the United States.

of fire prevention, it let its residents know that firefighters do more than put out fires—they also prevent them. Realizing the lifesaving potential of fire education, the Austin Fire Department decided to take an active fire prevention stance.

First, the department divided up the city into a number of geographical areas. Census information for each district was used to draw up a neighborhood profile. The firefighters coordinated the statistical information with the specific fire problems of the various areas and tailored an education program for each district. Then, a fire department education officer met with community leaders in each district to discuss their neighborhood's particular fire problems. Each community leader was asked to share the message with others in the neighborhood.

The department also experimented with home visits to inspect private residences for fire hazards. Fire safety literature was developed for distribution to local business owners and managers.

The main key to the department's success has been its media and marketing methodology. Austin's effort is extraordinarily aggressive. Under the sponsorship of the fire department, fire safety messages are flashed on theater screens in local moviehouses. Fire safety messages also appear on billboards.

The local media participate heavily in fire education. Public service announcements appear regularly on local television and radio stations. The media broadcast special programs during Austin's annual Fire Prevention Week. Although some spots are contributed by the media, the fire department also buys time to air fire safety messages. Live video cable shows are used to get the word out, and firefighters make regular appearances on local radio talk shows. The local Fox station's "Kids Club" show airs fire safety messages year-round. In addition, firefighters make regular visits to local schools, especially at the elementary level.

The more than 700 Austin firefighters participate in public education activities on a daily basis. Most recently, the fire department has been developing sophisticated ways of tracking the effectiveness of its fire safety programs. As budget axes fall, the department knows that these data are necessary to the survival of its programs.

COBB COUNTY, GEORGIA: DEFYING DEATH

Since Cobb County borders on Atlanta, people here enjoy the benefits of a major urban center as well as the tranquility of life in the wooded hills of northern Georgia. Located on the Chattahoochee River, Cobb County encompasses both farmland and high-rise office parks, ranging from the tiny community of Acworth to Dobbins Air Force Base.

Between 1971 and 1990, Cobb County's population more than doubled. Fewer than 200,000 people lived in the county at the beginning of the 70s. By 1990, almost half a million people called Cobb County home. Although such explosive population growth is not unusual in the United States, Cobb County's fire statistics are extraordinary. While the population was skyrocketing, the county's fire rate went down. Even though Cobb County's population had more than doubled, the fire district reported fewer fires in 1990 than in 1971. Following standard statistical profiles, Cobb County was projected to have almost 8,000 fires in 1990, yet it had under 1,500—about a thousand fewer fires than were reported in 1971 (Figure 12-3).

How did they do it? What was it about this department that led

 The fire death rate in hotels and motels has dropped dramatically thanks to the widespread use of sprinklers.

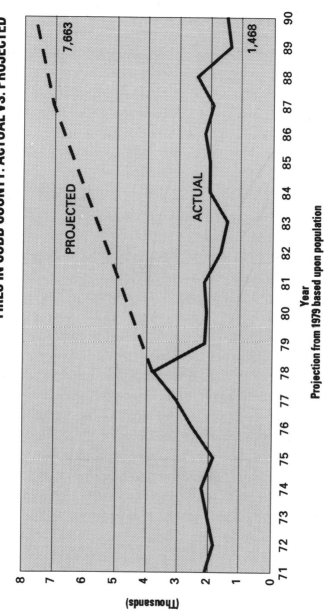

Figure 12-3.

FIRES IN COBB COUNTY: ACTUAL VS. PROJECTED

Source: Cobb County Fire and Emergency Services

it to be selected the outstanding fire department in the United States in 1988 by the U.S. Fire Administration?

There were many factors contributing to its success, but most significantly, it was the decision to focus firefighting efforts on prevention. In the words of Fire Chief David Hilton, ''There are other ways to put out a fire besides putting the wet stuff on the red stuff.''

When Cobb County started its fire safety campaign, it employed 62 firefighters, most of whom were funded by the federal Comprehensive Employment and Training Act (CETA) employment program. Beginning in 1975, these federally funded salaries gradually became funded by the Cobb County Fire Department, and the firefighters were given an intensive, three-week training course. Two training division positions were added. In 1976, county fire personnel were given specific training in fire codes and ordinances. The county encouraged more cooperation between county building inspectors and the fire department; it also standardized the two groups' requirements for certificates of occupancy. The next year, Cobb County committed itself to teaching fire safety at the fifth-grade level in all its public schools.

Over the years, more training instructors were hired, home inspections increased, and an arson division was added. New ordinances required permits for fireplace installation. An intensive inspection program for multifamily dwellings was introduced. A residential smoke detector ordinance was passed. More educational programs were introduced, starting at the kindergarten level.

Cobb County also introduced a voluntary sprinkler law for multifamily and single-family housing that encourages installation in homes by offering trade-offs such as reduced fire rating requirements for building materials. As Colonel Nathan Wilson of the Cobb County Fire Department describes it, the idea is to make fire education more than just a message for schoolchildren. It also

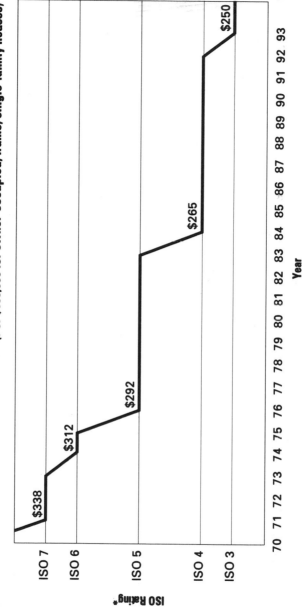

Figure 12-4.
COBB COUNTY HOMEOWNERS' INSURANCE PREMIUMS
(Per $100,000 for owner-occupied, frame, single-family houses)

*ISO—Insurance Services Office—rating is roughly equivalent to safety level. In 1970, with an ISO rating of 10, the insurance rate would have been $600.

Source: Cobb County Fire and Emergency Services

153

means educating builders and homeowners to the advantages of fire prevention planning.

The fire department's experience has shown that the expense of sprinklers, especially when installed at the time of construction, can be offset by tradeoffs that ultimately benefit the consumer. For example, fewer fire hydrants are needed in front of buildings with sprinkler systems, whether they are apartment complexes, multifamily homes, or single-family homes. In addition, when sprinklers are installed, rates for fire insurance fall substantially. In Cobb County, fire risk is so low, the average homeowner's fire insurance rate went from $338 per $100,000 valuation in 1971 to $250 in 1990 (Figure 12-4).

Currently, the public education division of Cobb County employs 14 part-time and five full-time staff members—a cadre that concentrates on stopping fires before they start.

Like Austin and Portland, Cobb County thinks fire safety. The collective experience of all these communities has proven the old saw that an ounce of prevention is worth a pound of cure.

13

Testing What You've Learned

What would you do if there was a fire in your home? How well is your home protected from fire? Do you know how to ensure the safety of your family in case of a fire? Test your fire safety quotient by taking this quiz. Answers appear following the quiz.

FIRE SAFETY QUIZ

1. What's the best way to prepare your family for a fire in the home?

2. What time of day is a fire in your home most likely to occur?

3. What part of the home is the best place to use as a meeting place for the family in case of a fire?

4. You discover a fire in your home in the middle of the night. What do you do first?

5. If your family has to flee a fire in your home, should they leave the house individually or all together?

6. What's the worst thing you can do in a fire?

7. How many serious fire emergencies is a person likely to encounter in a lifetime?

8. What valuables should you collect from your home before you escape a fire?

9. What's the single most important piece of equipment for surviving a fire?

10. What simple act can you perform when escaping a fire to help save lives and property?

11. When making up your fire escape plan, how many exits should you have from each room in your home?

12. What's the number one cause of residential fires?

13. What's the number one cause of residential fire deaths?

14. You've just had a party in your home and all the guests have left. What should you do before you go to bed?

15. What's the proper way to empty an ashtray?

16. How long can a cigarette smolder in a piece of furniture?

17. How do most people who die in a fire succumb?

18. Which two age groups are most likely to die in a fire?

19. Which age group is most likely to be injured in a fire?

20. At what age are children most likely to play with matches and start a fire that will kill them?

21. How much higher is the death rate from fires in the United States compared to most other nations?

22. What two drugs are most often linked to fires?

23. Which type of home is twice as likely as the average home to experience a fire?

24. You discover a small fire burning in your home. How long do you have to extinguish the fire before fleeing?

25. It's the middle of the night, the smoke detector sounds, and you wake up to the smell of smoke. What should you do?

26. You are trying to escape a fire, but you discover the door of your room is hot. What do you do?

27. How will smoke affect you if you are sleeping?

28. Outside the home, where are you most likely to die in a fire?

29. What type of fire extinguisher should you use to put out an electrical fire?

30. How can improper fuses cause a fire?

31. When is an electrical cord a fire hazard?

32. Everyone knows that a stack of dry newspapers is a fire hazard. But why is a stack of wet newspapers also a fire danger?

33. Why is a dirty chimney a fire hazard?

34. What should you do if your clothes catch on fire?

35. Your clothes catch on fire at the hemline. How long does it take fire to go from there to your neck?

36. Carbon monoxide is one of the most toxic gases created by a fire. What happens when you breathe it?

37. Why should gasoline always be stored in a tightly covered container?

38. You discover a large fire in your house. A fire extinguisher is nearby. What do you do next?

39. While working on an upper floor of a high-rise, you notice smoke coming in beneath the door. What should you do?

40. Why should the elevator never be used to escape a fire?

41. If you are trapped in a high-rise fire, should you climb to the roof or descend to the ground floor?

42. While attempting to escape a fire, you enter a smoke-filled hallway. What do you do?

43. You are attempting to escape a fire, but you are unable to open the window. What should you do?

44. You are trapped in a high-rise that has a fire burning on a lower floor. What do you do?

45. You are forced to jump from a burning building into a safety net. In what position should you land on the net?

46. If you call the fire department to report a fire, what critical information should you give them?

47. You pull the alarm at an outside fire box to report an emergency. What do you do next?

48. What's the worst thing you can do in case of a grease fire?

49. Besides the stove and oven, what other kitchen fixture represents the greatest fire hazard?

50. You smell a gas leak, but you can't determine its source. Why would it be dangerous to search for the leak with a flashlight?

ANSWERS TO QUIZ

1. Practice fire drills to make sure that everyone in the household knows what to do in case of a fire, including which escape routes to use for every room in the home.

2. Most fires occur between midnight and 8 A.M.

3. No area inside the home should be used as an emergency meeting place. Always designate an area outside the home as a place for everyone to gather.

4. Wake up the other members of the household and tell them to get out because there's a fire.

5. Everyone should leave the home individually and gather at the designated emergency meeting place outside the home. Waiting for others inside the home may lead to unnecessary injury or even death.

6. Panic. Panic is a waste of energy that can result in death.

7. The odds are that each of us will encounter three serious fire emergencies over the course of a lifetime.

8. Never try to collect any valuables before escaping your home. The seconds you use to look for your wallet or mementos may mean the difference between life and death.

9. A smoke detector is your first line of defense because it gives you a warning in time to escape.

10. Always close the door behind you. It will delay the spread of flames and deadly smoke.

11. You should have two ways to exit every room in your home.

12. The number one cause of residential fires is defective heating systems. Cooking-related accidents is number two.

13. Careless smoking is the number one cause of fires that result in death.

14. Look in between the furniture cushions to ensure that no cigarettes have been left smoldering. Then empty the ashtrays properly.

15. Ashtrays should be emptied into metal containers and covered with a tight-fitting lid.

16. Cigarettes can smolder in a piece of furniture for three or four hours before bursting into flame.

17. About 90 percent of fire deaths are caused by smoke and poisonous gases in combination with flames.

18. The very young—especially children under age 5—and the elderly—particularly those over 75—are the two age groups at greatest risk.

19. Young men between the ages of 15 and 24 are the age group most likely to be injured by fires, mostly because they spend a lot of time in gasoline-related activities and they are often reckless and careless. Because of their youth and agility, they will probably escape the fire before it kills them.

20. The average age of children killed in fires started by playing with matches is three.

21. Fifty to 100 percent higher.

22. Tobacco and alcohol. Careless smoking combined with drinking is a deadly combination.

23. Mobile homes are twice as likely as the average home to experience a serious fire.

24. If you can't extinguish a fire within 30 seconds, flee the scene.

25. Don't sit up in bed or stand up in the room. The smoke at that level might kill you. Roll out of bed and crawl to the door.

26. Don't open the door. Seek an alternative exit. If you are trapped in the room, stuff blankets, towels, sheets, or newspapers around the edge of the door to keep out smoke. Go to a window, open it slightly, and signal your location to those outside.

27. The smoke will not wake you up. It will put you into a deeper sleep.

28. In your automobile.

29. A dry-chemical BC or ABC fire extinguisher should be used for electrical fires.

30. Wiring is made to carry an exact electrical power load. Fuses are designed to blow when that load is exceeded. Improper fuses can bring excess power into the wiring, causing overheating and eventually a fire.

31. Frayed or cracked electrical cords are always dangerous. They also represent a potential danger when the wire is hung over a nail, run under a rug, when it is wet, or when it is overloaded.

32. The decomposing wet newspapers undergo a chemical reaction that generates heat and can cause spontaneous combustion.

33. A clogged chimney can choke off the air necessary for proper ventilation. Also, the soot itself can catch on fire.

34. Stop, drop to the ground, and roll back and forth until the fire is out. If a blanket or rug is within reach, grab it and wrap it around you to smother the flames.

35. Fire can travel from the hemline to the neckline in 10 seconds or less.

36. Carbon monoxide acts like an extremely powerful anesthetic. First it makes you woozy, then disoriented. Next it causes you to pass out, then it kills you—all within a matter of seconds.

37. Gasoline fumes are heavier than air. When gas is stored in an improperly sealed container, the fumes creep along the ground. If they reach a heat source, such as the flame of a water heater, the fumes can explode into flames.

38. Never try to put out a large fire, even with a fire extinguisher. If you can, close the door to the room where the fire is burning, and use the time you have to escape.

39. Stuff something around the doorjamb to keep out the smoke. Cover air-conditioning or heating ducts if smoke is seeping in. If there is a phone in the room, call the fire department (or dial 911). Open the window partially and hang a cloth outside or make some noise to signal your location. If you're on a high floor, don't jump. Chances are the door will protect you from the fire until help arrives.

40. Many elevators are designed to respond to heat. If you get on an elevator in a burning building, it may take you to a floor where there's a fire. Also, the elevator can act like a chimney and become a smoke-filled death trap. Always use the stairs instead.

41. Always descend the stairs. Only go to the roof as a last resort.

42. First, seek an alternative escape route. If none exists, drop to your knees or stomach and crawl to the exit.

43. Don't open the window, unless you have to. Break the window only as a last resort. Use a chair or other piece of furniture to smash it. Make sure that the doorway is secure against smoke or gases. If you break the

window, you may cause a flood of poisonous fumes to pour into the room.

44. Exit via the stairwell. If it is filled with smoke, return to your floor and seal off your room from smoke. Notify the fire department of your location and wait for help.

45. If you are forced to jump into a safety net, try to land in a sitting position.

46. Stay on the line long enough to give the fire department all the information they request. The most critical information is the exact location and street address of the fire.

47. Stay next to the box and wait until the fire department arrives so that you can direct them to the fire.

48. Never try to douse the flames with water, which will spread the flames rather than extinguish the fire. Instead, you should cover the flames with a pot lid, use a BC or ABC fire extinguisher, or throw baking soda on the fire.

49. The kitchen exhaust fan can cause a fire when the buildup of grease and dust reacts with the heat of the motor.

50. When there is a gas leak, any spark can cause an explosion. Everyone knows that it would be stupid to light a match while looking for a leak, but it can be just as deadly to click on a flashlight or even an overhead light. When you smell a gas leak and don't know its source, ventilate the area, leave immediately, and call the fire department.

EPILOGUE. FIREFIGHTERS, THE TRUE HEROES AMONG US

Firefighting is one of the most dangerous occupations to be involved in, yet it is necessary for survival. Men and women face the violence of fire throughout this country thousands of time a day. Many times the odds are so great, they themselves almost concede defeat. If it weren't for their guts and tremendous desire to conquer that fire, our cities and communities would only be ashes by now.

—The Unpaid Professional—The Volunteer Firefighter, by
ANDY STEINMULLER, DIRECTOR OF FIRE SAFETY AND EDUCATION,
NASSAU COUNTY FIRE MARSHAL'S OFFICE

Starting with the days when Peter Stuyvesant, the first governor of New Amsterdam (which eventually became New York), distributed leather buckets to the citizenry to help protect the city from fire, Americans have a long and proud tradition of volunteer firefighting.

Today, there are over three million firefighters in the United States, and most of them are volunteers. Their selfless work has saved countless lives and prevented untold injury. In a time when the word "hero" is used for everyone from sports stars to convicted felons, volunteer firefighters are the real McCoy. They represent the best aspirations of the human spirit—true heroes who make a life-and-death difference in their own communities.

Ready to go at a moment's notice, whether it's the middle of the night, early Sunday morning, or even Christmas Eve, these brave men and women are always prepared to save lives. Some of them have made the ultimate sacrifice for their neighbors. Every year, about 100 firefighters die in the line of duty; about half of them are volunteers. Additionally, 60,000 firefighters are injured annually; again, half of them are volunteers.

After the fire is out, the volunteer's job is still not done. He or she must return to the firehouse to do the paperwork, describing what happened for the official record. The equipment used in the fire also has to be kept clean and repaired. There's nothing glamorous about washing tires or rolling up firehoses when you're dead tired from spending the evening putting out a blaze, but it has to be done. It's also part of the job.

When they're not fighting fires, these dedicated volunteers spend their spare time studying new methods of fire suppression or learning how to handle the latest equipment. And all of it on their own time, usually in addition to their regular jobs. Volunteer firefighters do not sleep late on the weekends. While the rest of us are relaxing, these men and women—for reasons most people can't begin to fathom—spend their weekend mornings sharpening their fire-fighting expertise or learning first aid techniques, because it's the only time that most of them have free.

Because budgets are tight, many communities not only cannot afford salaries for professional firefighters, they can't even pay for firefighting equipment. So, in addition to volunteering for a task that risks life and limb, members of small fire departments also have to raise the money to pay for their equipment. They organize pancake breakfasts, raffles, barbecues—whatever it takes to get the money to keep the community safe. Even in large cities, volunteers often help make neighborhoods a better place to live by giving their time to educate the public or raise funds for fire prevention.

And volunteers often have to deal with a lot more than fires. When a flood threatens, the volunteer firefighter can be counted on to be on the front line, throwing down sandbags. When a blizzard strikes, the volunteer firefighter is there with shovel, snowplow, or any other implement available to lend a helping hand. Tornados, hurricanes—any emergency that a community might face—brings out the volunteer firefighter.

It's not just communitywide emergencies either. In many small towns, the local fire department also serves as the emergency medical service, handling everything from drug overdoses to delivering babies. Sometimes they render first aid, sometimes they save a life—and sometimes they just reassure a frightened child.

Volunteer firefighters join their local departments out of desire, but most volunteer fire departments are started out of necessity, because the community does not have the means to hire a team of full-time firefighters. But even though volunteer firefighters aren't paid professionals, there's nothing amateur about their work. As Chief Andy Steinmuller of New York's Nassau County Fire Department says, volunteers are ''unpaid professionals.''

If you ask the volunteers why they do it, you'll get a variety of answers—to help the community, to use their free time productively, to meet other members of the community. Whatever the reason, volunteering to serve as a firefighter is one of the bravest and most selfless activities anyone can undertake. And thank God so many people choose to do it.

APPENDIX. MAJOR U.S. FIRES OF THE 20TH CENTURY

1903 Rhodes Opera House, Boyertown, Pennsylvania—
170 killed

1903 Iroquois Theatre, Chicago, Illinois—602 killed

1908 Lakeview Grammar School, Collinwood, Ohio—
175 killed

1911 Triangle Shirtwaist Factory, New York City, New York—
145 killed

1923 Cleveland School, Beulah, South Carolina—77 killed

1928 Bond Dance Hall, West Plains, Missouri—38 killed

1929 Cleveland Clinic, Cleveland, Ohio—125 killed

1930 Ohio State Penitentiary, Columbus, Ohio—320 killed

1931 Home for the Aged, Pittsburgh, Pennsylvania—48 killed

1936 Terminal Hotel, Atlanta, Georgia—32 killed

1940 Rhythm Club, Natchez, Mississippi—207 killed

1942 Coconut Grove Nightclub, Boston, Massachusetts—
492 killed

1943 Forrest Park Sanitarium, Seattle, Washington—32 killed

1943 Gulf Motel, Houston, Texas—54 killed

1946 LaSalle Hotel, Chicago, Illinois—61 killed

1946 Winecoff Hotel, Atlanta, Georgia—119 killed

1949 St. Anthony Hospital, Effingham, Illinois—74 killed

1950 Mercy Hospital, Davenport, Iowa—41 killed

1953 Littlefield Nursing Home, Largo, Florida—35 killed

1955 Barton Hotel, Chicago, Illinois—29 killed

1957 Katie Jane Memorial Home for the Aged, Warrenton,
Missouri—72 killed

1957 Council Bluffs Convalescent Home, Council Bluffs, Iowa—
13 killed

1958 Our Lady of Angels Grade School, Chicago, Illinois—
95 killed

1961 Thomas Hotel, San Francisco, California—20 killed

1963 Surfside Hotel, Atlantic City, New Jersey—25 killed

1963 Roosevelt Hotel, Jacksonville, Florida—22 killed

1967 Dale's Penthouse Restaurant, Montgomery, Alabama—
25 killed

1968 Randolph Tavern, Moberly, Missouri—13 killed

1970 Nursing Home, Marietta, Ohio—31 killed

1970 Ozark Hotel, Seattle, Washington—20 killed

1970 Point Square Hotel, Los Angeles, California—19 killed

1970 Pioneer Hotel, Tucson, Arizona—28 killed

1971 Nursing Home, Honesdale, Pennsylvania—15 killed

1973 Cocktail Lounge, New Orleans, Louisiana—32 killed

1973 Apartment House, Los Angeles, California—25 killed

1973 Galey Nursing Home, Wayne, Pennsylvania—15 killed

1974 Gulliver's Disco, Port Chester, New York—24 killed

1974 Washington House Hotel, Berkeley Springs, West Virginia—12 killed

1975 Seminole County Jail, Sanford, Florida—11 killed

1976 Pathfinder Hotel, Fremont, Nebraska—20 killed

1976 Winecrest Nursing Home, Chicago, Illinois—24 killed

1976 Social Club, Bronx, New York—25 killed

1977 Stratford Hotel, Breckenridge, Minnesota—16 killed

1977 Beverly Hills Nightclub, Southgate, Kentucky—164 killed

1977 Maury County Jail, Columbia, Tennessee—42 killed

1978 Coates House Hotel, Kansas City, Missouri—20 killed

1978 Allen Motor Inn, Honesdale, Pennsylvania—20 killed

1978 Tenement, Newark, New Jersey—12 killed

1978 Mental Hospital, Ellisville, Mississippi—15 killed

1980 Boarding House, Bradley Beach, New Jersey—14 killed

1980 MGM Grand Hotel, Las Vegas, Nevada—85 killed

1980 Stouffer's Inn, Harrison, New York—26 killed

1981 Beachview Rest Home, Keansburg, New Jersey—31 killed

1982 Westchase Hilton, Houston, Texas—12 killed

1982 Pinter Hotel, Hoboken, New Jersey—13 killed

1982 Dorothy Mae Apartment Hotel, Los Angeles, California—24 killed

1982 Biloxi Jail, Biloxi, Mississippi—29 killed

1983 Home for the Mentally Handicapped, Annandale Village, Georgia—8 killed

1984 Elliot Chambers Rooming Home, Beverly, Massachusetts—14 killed

1984 Alexander Hamilton Hotel, Paterson, New Jersey—14 killed

1986 Dupont Plaza Hotel, San Juan, Puerto Rico—97 killed

1989 Hillhaven Nursing Home, Norfolk, Virginia—12 killed

1989 John Sevier Retirement Center, Johnson City, Tennessee—16 killed

1990 Happy Land Social Club, Bronx, New York—87 killed

1990 Fontana Hotel, Miami, Florida—9 killed

Source: National Fire Sprinkler Association

STATES THAT REQUIRE SMOKE DETECTORS IN ONE- AND TWO-FAMILY DWELLINGS (1992)

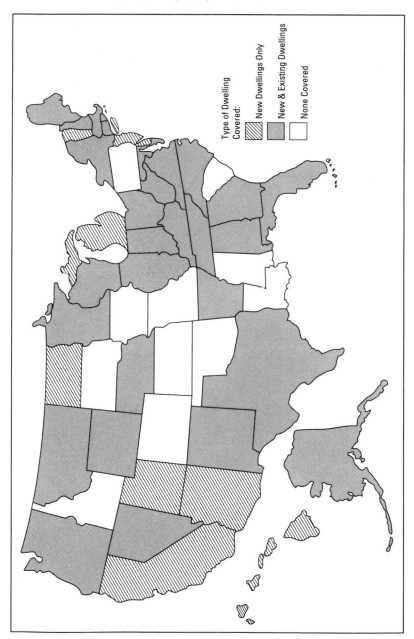

Source: First Alert

GLOSSARY

ARSON The malicious act of setting a property, such as a building or vehicle, on fire. Under this definition, the cause for setting the fire can be for money, sexual gratification, anger, or revenge. More narrowly defined, the term is used to describe a fire that is set for fraudulent purposes, such as receiving fire insurance payments.

BACKDRAFT This is a phenomenon that occurs when a room that is superheated by a fire is suddenly exposed to a fresh influx of oxygen, such as when a window or door is inadvertently opened. When the oxygen is added, the room erupts into flame.

CARBON MONOXIDE (CO) The extremely toxic gas that is produced by fire. It is colorless and odorless, and it quickly debilitates anyone who breathes it. It is the result of carbon that has not been completely burned during the fire. Once airborne, it enters the lungs and replaces oxygen in the bloodstream. The effects of breathing carbon monoxide are disorientation, dizziness, drowsiness, asphyxiation, and eventually death.

CURIOUS CHILD FIRE SETTER A child who begins a fire simply out of curiosity. The child is usually fascinated by fire and wants to experience the starting of a fire. The child is generally under the age of 10 and as young as three years old. The curious child fire setter normally sets only one fire. The curious child fire setter is in direct contrast to the problem child fire setter.

FEDERAL EMERGENCY MANAGEMENT AGENCY (FEMA) Begun during the administration of President Jimmy Carter, FEMA is the umbrella federal department that handles national emergencies, from hurricanes to fire control. It is the department that oversees the U.S. Fire Administration.

FIRE A chemical reaction that occurs when sufficient amounts of heat, oxygen, and fuel combine. The phenomenon of combustion will fail if any of the three ingredients of the chemical reaction is removed.

FIRE LOAD Objects that burn, such as the upholstery or furniture in a home. A place with a high fire load has a greater risk of damage from fire than an area with a low fire load.

FLAMEPROOF Fabric, furniture, clothing, or other items that resist catching on fire even when exposed to direct flame. Any of these items, however, usually ignite after an extended exposure to flames.

FLAME-RETARDANT Fabric, furniture, clothing, or other items that have been treated to avoid catching on fire when exposed to limited amounts of heat or flames. Items that are flame-retardant are more likely to catch on fire than items that are flameproof, but they are more resistant than untreated textiles, furniture, or clothing.

FLASHOVER What happens when a fire reaches a temperature hot enough to set everything, including smoke itself, on fire.

FLASH POINT The temperature at which a substance will catch on fire. The flash point varies widely depending on the combustible; the flashpoint of diesel fuel is 100°F, but for gasoline it's −45°F.

INCENDIARY FIRE Any fire that is suspicious in nature, such as arson. This category also includes fires started by children playing with matches and fires started by pyromaniacs.

ISO RATING The Insurance Services Office, headquartered in New York, provides a wide range of advisory, rating, actuarial, statistical, and other services. The ISO Rating is roughly equivalent to the safety level of a building. It is used by insurance companies to determine the cost of fire insurance premiums.

NATIONAL FIRE INCIDENTS REPORTING SYSTEM (NFIRS) A state-by-state tally that tracks where fires begin, their cause, and their effect. The system is used to develop fire prevention and suppression policies.

PROBLEM CHILD FIRE SETTER A child who starts fires in reaction to emotional or psychological difficulties. In the vast majority of cases, the child is male and has a history of setting fires.

PYROMANIA A rare psychological pathology associated with an uncontrollable urge to set fires.

PYROMANIAC A person so obsessed with fires that he or she is driven to set them. Only about five percent of all purposely set fires are started by pyromaniacs.

TRAILER Flammable material, often a liquid, used by an arsonist to lead a trail from the point of ignition to the room or object he or she wants to burn.

U.S. FIRE ADMINISTRATION The federal agency that oversees national fire prevention and control policies. Among its duties are the nationwide collection of fire data and the dissemination of information on fire prevention and control.

INDEX

ABOUT THE AUTHORS

Dr. Frank Field is senior meteorologist and senior health and science editor at WCBS-TV in New York City. With 35 years in television news, Dr. Field has developed a reputation for consistently bringing vital health and science information to the public. His 15-part series, "Plan to Get Out Alive," which was broadcast in October, 1987, won six Emmy awards for Outstanding Health and Science Programming and Outstanding Community Outreach and is credited with saving many lives.

Dr. Field, a graduate of Brooklyn College, Columbia University, and the Massachusetts College of Optometry, has received four honorary doctorate degrees. Married for 45 years, he has three grown children and three grandchildren.

John Morse is an artist and writer living in New York City. Formerly senior editor at Fairchild Publications, he began his journalism career in 1971. He has worked as a reporter and editor in New York, Oregon, Florida, and Spain, served as a writer for the Travel Channel, and was editor in chief for U.S. Business Press. His collages have appeared on book covers and in *Mademoiselle, Advertising Age,* and *Egg* magazine. Several of his works have been displayed at the Socrates Sculpture Park in New York City.